A STICK, HILL BOOTS
AND A GOOD COLLIE DOG

Ben Coutts' previous books include:

Bothy to Big Ben
Auld Acquaintance
A Scotsman's War
Bred in the Highlands

All are available from Mercat Press

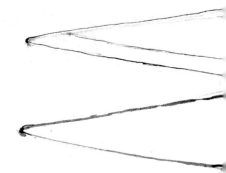

A STICK, HILL BOOTS AND A GOOD COLLIE DOG

A Shepherd's Life Fifty Years Ago

BEN COUTTS

Illustrations by
Maisie Murray

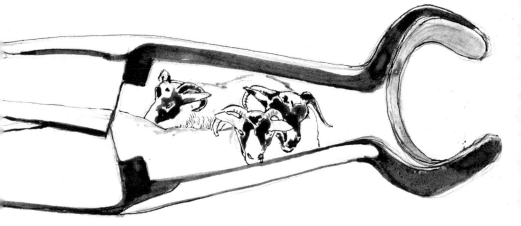

MERCAT
PRESS

First published in 1999 by Mercat Press
James Thin, 53 South Bridge, Edinburgh EH1 1YS

ISBN 1873644 876

Typeset in Bembo at Mercat Press
Printed and bound in Great Britain by
Redwood Books, Trowbridge, Wiltshire

Contents

Illustrations

The ink-drawings at the openings of chapters are by Maisie Murray

The 'Three Musketeers'—Donald MacPherson, Ben Coutts and Pat MacNab.

Author's Preface

Since biblical times, when 'shepherds watched their flocks by night' etc., a shepherd's life has been seen as having something idyllic about it. People send home postcards from all those places round the Mediterranean showing an old man in front of his flock of sheep, or watch 'One Man and His Dog' on T.V. thinking that they are watching shepherds enjoying their hobby—which couldn't be further from the truth, but of that later. And of course this idyllic picture is helped by the fact that shepherds have usually lived in the most lovely parts of our island, be it the Highlands, the Borders, the Lake District, the Welsh hills and the South Downs where I was lucky enough to shepherd for a short spell. Then there are the eastern counties of the country, counties like Norfolk and Suffolk. Suffolk is famous to this day for the breed of sheep it produced, which is still the best terminal sire we have in this country, although it has had to face fierce opposition from imported breeds.

Sadly, today the shepherd's life is no longer so idyllic. In my half century of farming I have probably seen more changes than have occurred at any other time in history. This period began after the Second World War with the advent of the tractor as opposed to the horse. In my opinion the greatest gifts to farming brought by new developments were, first, electricity (no more taking out a paraffin hurricane lamp to see if a cow was calving, you just touched a switch). Then came three-point linkage on a tractor, so that no longer did one have manually to lift harrows etc. as the tractor did it for you. But as far as shepherding is concerned I don't think these technological innovations have helped. Oh, I know a shepherd can get round his flock on a four-wheeled motorbike quicker than his forebears did on foot, but he doesn't 'ken' his sheep as thoroughly as they did.

It is on the medical side that shepherds have gained in the last fifty years. Problems like the dreaded 'loupin ill', liver fluke, worms and abortion have been controlled thanks to the efforts of our research workers.

My hope in writing this book is that the average town dweller might be interested to learn what a shepherd's life was like before the advent of all the modern vehicles and medications etc. that have been introduced to ease his work. I thought the best way of showing this would be to describe the shepherd's year month by month. To help me remember those old days I have called on my old boss and friend, Pat MacNab, and Donald MacPherson. Pat went full-time shepherding after we had been pony boys together on a grouse moor in 1935, whereas I went more into the managerial side of sheep farming, and one of my head shepherds was Donald.

As 'oldies' our main worry is that, because everyone now wants a higher standard of living than we enjoyed in our younger days, few sons and daughters of hill farmers and shepherds are following in their fathers' footsteps. You need only to go to one of the major sheep sales in this country and look around at the assembled company of buyers and sellers to see that barely five per cent are below the age of fifty, if not sixty! This eventually is going to have a devastating effect on the hill country as we know it. Perhaps the reason this situation has come about is that our shepherds were not appreciated as they should have been for the hard job they had to do. It is that hard job that we hope to portray in this book.

Acknowledgements

It is hard indeed to know who to thank most for the help I've received in writing this book. But because my sister, Maisie, suffered a stroke during the time she was completing the sketches which I think are the making of this book, I'm thanking her first.

What fun I have had renewing my friendships with Pat and Donald. I wish to thank them for their sage advices, which, unlike Tam o' Shanter, I have not despised!

To Polly Pullar, who lent me some super photos, and, as a professional photographer, could have charged me an arm and a leg for them, but didn't, my thanks.

To the faithful quartet who have helped me with all my books, my thanks. To Sal, for her constant backing up and general enthusiasm for the project. To Isabel, for her immaculate typing and promptness, never being late in churning out the next chapter. And to Tom and Seán of the Mercat Press who, when I said I'd written my last book, replied: 'Nonsense, there's another in you yet!' Whether they were right or not I leave to the readers to judge.

And finally, my thanks to my good friend, Dan Buglass, the leading Scots agricultural journalist. He has been more than kind in his reviews of my previous books, just as he has been in the Foreword to this one.

To all the above my best thanks.

Foreword

By Dan Buglass

There will never be another Ben Coutts. He is unique in the annals of Scottish rural history. Now into his eighties, Ben remains as astutely aware of all that is happening in the countryside as ever. That comes as no surprise, given his long and wide-ranging experience over all those years.

Ben was born a son of the manse with a father and mother who wished their family to be, first, happy in life, and then successful. They were fortunate in their aspirations, though Ben initially disappointed their ambitions for him by failing to enter the veterinary profession. That loss was agriculture's gain.

From shepherd to pony boy, and then to a distinguished soldier who suffered heroic injuries which were endured with a stoicism that has never deserted him, Ben progressed to estate manager, then farmer in his own right and secretary of the Aberdeen-Angus Cattle Society. There was much more too along the way that enriched his own life and, more importantly, all who came to know him.

I have grown to know him over the last thirty years. At first he was held in something approaching awe, but that blossomed into an enduring friendship which transcends the difference in years. As a broadcaster of longstanding repute his style was always blunt and to the point. He says exactly what is in his mind. The same holds true for his several books beginning with *Bothy to Big Ben*. It was an instant success. Subsequent writings were equally fascinating.

This latest book is perhaps the most poignant of all in that it is one of the very few covering the art, and it is a real art, of shepherding and the people of the hills and glens. As a native Borderer I feel a special empathy with the subject and can personally relate to Ben's time in the Ettrick Valley. It is a very special place, beloved of James Hogg, Walter Scott and William Wordsworth.

Hogg himself over 200 years ago penned his 'Shepherd's Guide'. It still reads well. The thoughts and memories of Ben Coutts among the hills and sheep are equally compelling.

The Song of the Shepherd

Oh the lambing time's in April,
And the couping time's in June,
The dipping time's in August,
And the speaning time is soon.
Be it Sunday, be it holiday,
The shepherd's never done,
And he doesnae rise at eight o' clock,
He rises wi' the sun.

Oh, the mists are slowly lifting
Frae the top o' Tinto Hill,
And the shepherd who is standing there
Drinks in the quiet and still.
He is gathering for the clipping,
And awaits the light o' day,
And wi' the rising o' the sun
He'll start his weary way.

Oh, there's twinning, there is dipping,
And there's marking wi' the keel,
There is dressing ready for the sales,
And feeding hay and meal.
There is udderlucking bad anes,
Oh, the battle's never won,
And the shepherd's day is started
Wi' the rising o' the sun.

It's a life of dedication,
And the money's often poor,
Wi' his dogs as sole companions
He tramps miles across the moor.
But when the day is over,
And a' the work is done,
He beds wi' satisfaction
Till the rising o' the sun.

Oh the lambing time's in April,
And the couping time's in June,
The dipping time's in August,
And the speaning time is soon.
Be it Sunday, be it holiday,
The shepherd's never done,
And he doesnae rise at eight o' clock,
He rises wi' the sun.

Presented to Pat MacNab,
who herded Tinto,
by John Dickson, the Border Herd.

January

JANUARY has always been my least favourite month, as it is dark, usually wet or stormy and seems to go on for five weeks from Christmas to January 31st! For shepherds before the war, conditions depended where they were employed as, although we are small in area compared with other sheep-producing countries, our very varied terrain and climate mean that there are terrific differences in a shepherd's year from place to place.

During my spell in Sussex in the thirties the shepherds, with their Southdown breed of sheep, would be lambing in January to have lambs ready for the lucrative Easter market. What a labour-intensive job they had, constantly moving those hand-made hazel hurdles to give the ewes a clean patch of mangel wurzels. Those hurdles have now been superseded by electric fencing by the few who still bother to fold sheep on roots.

On those winter days, how I loved the cosy caravan of the shepherd of the estate on which I was employed as a groom/farm labourer. How I wish I had had the sense at the time to make notes of his experiences of the changes he'd seen in his day—but how was I to know, as a callow youth in my late teens, that I myself was to live to see the greatest changes in agriculture that will happen in anyone's lifetime? But there are three things I do remember from my visits to 'Shep's' caravan on the chalk South Downs in Sussex. The first one was that the

Southdown ewes were not so easy to lamb as the Cheviots I had lambed in Ettrick. Was it that they were too small in that essential passage through which the lamb must pass before it gives that first cough, a sound so beloved by all shepherds who, when they hear it, know they've got a live lamb? The second thing was that the old-fashioned English sheep dogs, like Shep himself, didn't move too fast, and certainly wouldn't have managed to gather a Border hirsel like a Border collie would. But it's a case of 'horses for courses', and a Border collie would be far too slick for sheep used to being moved slowly onto 'pastures new'—in this case a fresh patch of mangels. The third thing was what lambing was all about before the advent of in-wintering and closed-circuit T.V. covering the lambing shed—long nights and days.

This month in a shepherd's year needed, and still needs, some alcoholic help. In Sussex, where beer was the usual tipple (four pence old money in my day and pretty innocuous stuff at that), they brewed their own wines. Old Shep made his own parsnip wine which had a real kick in it, no wonder I used to visit him so often! I often wonder what happened to that cosy old caravan with its wee wood-burning stove that saved many a lamb's life. It could have told so many stories of a shepherd's life before the mechanised era, and of the scenes it had witnessed as it was pulled from place to place by a horse on its iron-rimmed wheels.

For shepherds in the Highland areas that I have known best—West Perthshire and Argyll—January and February were some of their best months. There was a saying among hill farmers and factors of hill estates: 'You get the tups in when the shepherds have sobered up after the New Year'. Wages were so bad for shepherds pre-war that for most of them the only bottle of whisky in their house all year would be at New Year, when they would 'first foot' their neighbours. Some were luckier and would be included in a New Year celebration run by the estate or farm which employed them. As a boy I was part of one of those never-to-be-forgotten New Year celebrations at the head of Glenartney in Perthshire. After a clay pigeon shooting match all and sundry were invited to a super meal, following which everyone, but everyone, had either to sing a song or recite something. I remember well being absolutely terrified before singing 'Bonnie Strathyre'. Little did I realise that it was to be the first performance of many in fifty years of broadcasting and public speaking. I also remember the Estate Manager, who was Master of Ceremonies, singing after each person performed, 'Jolly good song, jolly well sung, jolly good fellows every one, if you can beat it you're welcome to try, but just please remember the singer is dry!' And rightly the shepherds helped themselves liberally to whisky. Teetotallers (of which there were none except for laddies like me) were given port. No wonder I hardly know what lemonade tastes like, and as for water, so far as I am concerned, I wash in that!

The head shepherd in Glenartney then was Peter MacNab, whose son Pat helped me with this book. Peter was a natural with sheep dogs, which is a gift that sadly I haven't been given. He had a dog called Bob who, when a cut of ewes was gathered so that the tup could be separated would single out the tup and 'wear' it to Peter. I'd like to see some of the modern 'one man and his dog' collies work on a hill instead of a golf course, far less single out a tup from a bunch of ewes. After bringing the ewes in to separate the tups, many places used to dose their ewes for liver fluke. This in the old days was a messy business, but now is done with one jag of a needle.

The early part of the year could be a social time for shepherds, with a Burns Night and various dances. How those lads could dance! Many didn't have what were, in the thirties, called 'dancing pumps'—light slippers—but even in their tackety boots their sense of time could outshine many a modern shepherd, who thinks being a foot or two (or is it a metre nowadays?) away from his partner is dancing.

As I've said there are tremendous differences between areas as far as shepherding goes. Cheviot sheep, for instance, are found mainly on green hill land, so one finds them in the Borders from where they originated, and Caithness and Sutherland where they were introduced by Border farmers like the Elliott family. The Scottish blackface (numerically the largest breed in Great Britain) is found mainly on heather land, and is famous for its hardiness. How they have kept that trait beats me, when I consider the pampering their tups have had during the fifty years I've been involved with the breed. My old boss, a brilliant stocksman, Duncan Stewart of Millhills, was the prime mover of Ben Challum Ltd., a sheep farming company that ran eight thousand blackface ewes from Killin to West of Tyndrum. He sent me off to buy some rams and told me, 'Don't buy any of those overfed ones because they'll fall in the first hill drain thinking it's a trough'. Then in the late forties and early fifties one could go to Newton Stewart and buy hardy sheep that had had little, if any, hand feeding. But times have changed, and since 'beauty is in the eye of the beholder', all tup breeders now feed.

Many soft, overfed tups used to go to Oban and Dalmally, the better ones having gone to Perth, Lanark and Newton Stewart, and a lot of them were bought by shepherds or farm managers from the Islands. These were all too often ill-paid and had to make up their income with 'luckspennies' from vendors who were keen to get rid of their tups. As a result, for many years there was a saying that 'there was a boat load of tups went to Mull after the autumn Ram Sales but only a lorry load came back to the January Cast Tup Sale'. Luckily most farms in Mull are now well run and the island is no longer known as the home for Mad Majors and Dotty Doctors!

After the tups were brought in from the ewes any older ones who might be committing incest by covering their daughters would go off to the Cast Tup Sales in January. (Large sheep enterprises are lucky in this respect as they can swap tups around from hirsel to hirsel if a tup proves to be a good breeder.) When I managed the Ardkinglas Estate in Argyll, the old Glasgow Market, now long defunct, was a great place to sell cast tups as they were eagerly bid for by dealers operating for the Pakistani community.

Shepherds who made those lovely shepherd's crooks with ram's horn handles and hazel shanks used to get the horns from those cast tups. I was never a good stick maker but I did make one or two forty years ago. Now that all tups for sale are being fed one no longer can find the good hard-centred tups' horn: all have that white centre, a sure sign of heavy hand feeding, making them useless for stickmakers.

But back to the shepherd's life in January, and we come back to the terrific differences in what shepherds do in the months when they are not lambing, shearing or preparing for sale and selling their stock. For instance Pat MacNab shepherded in Lanarkshire for part of his long and varied life. He said one of his jobs in January was to take the breeks off the ewe hoggs. Now many readers, yes, even shepherds in distant northern areas, may have heard 'that you canna tak' the breeks off a Highlander'—but off ewe hoggs, that's a different matter! In those large tracts of damn-all but molinia and nardus grasses, boulders, some heather and bracken that comprise all too many Highland estates, one needs at least three acres to sustain a ewe for a year, which means that the replacement stock (the ewe lambs that become ewe hoggs the next year) have to be sent away to winter in a more congenial setting where there is some decent keep to make them grow. But in the better areas, like the bits of Lanarkshire where Pat was shepherding, and lots of the Border country with those lovely rolling green hills, the ewe hoggs can be wintered at home. However, to save their virginity from the rapacious tups (who might be their sire) they have to be 'breeked'. The breeks were squares of cloth made of tweed saved from the shepherd's old plus-fours, which all shepherds wore in pre-war days before the advent of jeans. The breeks had to be very carefully sewn over the vital part of the ewe hogg's anatomy. This was done with old-fashioned sack-needles which had been initially used to sew up grain and potato sacks made from jute. Why great care had to be used was because some wily old tups would use their

The author and his shepherd, Robbie McHardy, about to gather Gaskbeg hill.

horns or their feet to pull off the breeks so as 'to have their way' with the young four-legged virgins.

The 'hefting' in all the Border country is much more strict than in the wild north. A 'heft' of ewes would be about four score, and the division from heft to heft could be a burn or even a drain. As the ewe lambs followed their mothers from the day they were born they learnt to 'heft' to their own bit of ground. This made it handy for a shepherd seeing something amiss in a heft to gather it in without disturbing the rest of the hirsel (normally about five hundred ewes).

But for some herds January was the only month they could get off-time to themselves. There was the Burns Supper to be enjoyed and, as winters were harder pre-war, there could be the odd curling match. My introduction to the 'roarin' game' was at the head of Ettrick where the farm on which I had worked part-time had its own curling pond (as had many farms then, which shows how much harder our winters were in days of yore). Later I was invited back to play while on embarkation leave during that desperately hard winter of 1939-40. The outside game is so entirely different to the modern indoor game, the former needing some strength to lift and throw the stone, whereas in the latter most of the skill seems to involve the curler pushing the stone up the rink and in many cases going half-way up the rink with it! Both games need skills of different sorts, but the outside game suited most shepherds the best.

Having said that, when I went to factor the Ardkinglas Estate I had no trouble in getting a couple of rinks from the shepherds to curl indoors at Crossmyloof in Glasgow. I think the chance of a day off may have helped, and when our opponent was the redoubtable Captain MacRae of Balliemore, with his Otter Ferry rinks, I could have filled a bus! The reason behind this was that the gallant Captain owned a distillery, and he would bring along all too many bottles produced by it. These he used to place at each end of the rinks, hoping to paralyse or anaesthetise the opposition, which he did all too successfully.

The Captain was one of the great characters it's been my pleasure to meet in my long and happy life. He was captured by the Turks in Gallipoli in the First World War but made such a nuisance of himself they let him go! As one of the first pilots in the Royal Flying Corps (the forerunners of 'the first of the few' in the second war) he took a biplane and crash-landed it on his front lawn at Balliemore, where he enjoyed some leave until he was hauled over the coals by High Command. When I knew him in the fifties it was through curling and his other great love, shinty. He used to turn up each year to see the six-a-side shinty tournament at the Dalmally Show, for which I did the commentary, and I always got a (nearly Royal) command to partake 'a refresh' with the Captain who, I might say, always had a most attractive secretary as his driver! They don't breed his sort today.

'Make do and mend' was the old Army saying about maintaining the things on which one depends to do one's job. January and February were the months of make do and mend, when the ravages of the preceding year on fences, stone dykes, stells, paths, bridges and lambing parrocks were patched up. Sadly one sees all too many of those wonderfully built stone fanks being allowed to fall down as more modern metal or wooden ones are used. Oh! I know only too well how difficult some of those old stone fanks were to work in, and I've left a lot of skin from the backs of my hands on their rugged and often protruding stones, but they were a work of art and served their purpose for many more years than most modern ones will do. As to the paths and bridges which are an essential part of any hill farm or estate, I wonder if many of the 'right to roam' people realise how much it costs to keep them up. Floods, big and small, can play havoc with a hill path, and an extra big one can wash away a bridge (unless it was built by General Wade, of which there are still, after all these years, some super examples). I wonder if ramblers would be willing to pay for their right to roam on those paths so carefully maintained each year by shepherds and ghillies?

I can never understand why sheep stells were only built in the Borders. Being built in a circle they are a marvellous protection for sheep in snowy conditions, as there is always an area that is completely clear of snow, whereas if they were rectangular they could be completely buried in snow no matter which way the wind blew. I never shepherded in the Borders long enough to have to use a 'stell' in winter. However I did have the unique honour of going over the hill from Ettrick to a sale in Lockerbie, with lambs, back in the thirties, and the shepherd and I put the lambs in a 'stell' above Lockerbie before taking them down to the mart looking fresh and clean the next morning. I said it was an honour, as today we see lambs being loaded into vast-sized lorries and coming out the other end far from fresh, and often, depending on the weather, not all that clean.

How sad that material gain has taken over from craftsmanship, because that is what has happened. Shepherds were craftsmen in the way they looked after their five hundred ewe hirsel, knowing just about every one (or at least the awkward ones!) and seeing that their offspring were properly presented and sold. The old time shepherds' ewes were usually properly 'drawn' (i.e. put in lots that are the same in size and conformation), but now this is rarely done. No wonder the New Zealanders have taken over so much of the supermarket trade, because all their lambs are like peas out of a pod. Our 'oldies' could have done this too but they never got the chance, and nowadays the modern shepherd has so many other things to think about he has no hope of learning what the supermarkets want in their stores.

Among the big changes that my age-group has seen in the sheep trade, along with modern techniques and management, has been the introduction of many European breeds of sheep, as a result of which the whole breeding pattern as well as the breeds themselves have changed. In the years before the last war breeds like the Southdowns, Dorset Downs and other Down breeds supplied the lucrative Easter market and the months until August. Then the Blackface lambs came on in their big numbers, as well as the other hill lambs like the Swales, Lonks, and the Welsh lambs. When I used to do the sheep commentary at the Royal Smithfield Show I used to annoy the exhibitors of the wee Welsh hill breed by calling them the white mice! But I have a great admiration for that breed, which like the Herdwicks in the Lake District seem to survive on fresh air! The Cheviots have always been best marketed after a spell on better keep, and are excellent off a turnip break. But we had enough home-bred lamb to supply the market until the following late spring. It was then that New Zealand lamb came in and filled the gap until British lamb came on the market again. Nowadays supermarkets seem to have New Zealand lamb for an awful lot of the year. Having been in New Zealand on two occasions I realise what a wonderful country it is for sheep production with its climate, its famous New Zealand white clover and its dedicated stocksmen (many, I'm proud to say, descended from Scottish shepherds).

But in January as in every month in the year the shepherd is thinking of the number of lambs he can produce and sell profitably for his boss. With this in mind he may have drawn off some of the leaner older ewes to give them a bit of feed. Feeding hill ewes pre-1939 was almost unheard of whereas nowadays it's the norm.

I've always been a great believer in having cattle on a hill farm, as if there are only sheep, who are selective grazers, the old long rubbishy grasses become dominant whereas cattle take everything. And look where cattle have been held overnight in the great days of the Cattle Trysts of Crieff and Falkirk—these places are still green to this day, all those years on. Cattle dung breeds wee beasties that birds like, and the dung contains what grass needs—nitrogen, potash and phosphate—whereas sheep dung doesn't. Many shepherds in January had hill cows to feed. In the pre-war years these would be Highlands or Galloways or their crosses by a Shorthorn bull, but sadly post-war (and after all that is now half a century ago) hill farmers like many others have gone for short-term profit and one wouldn't know how half the hill cows are bred. 'Heinz 57 Varieties' I call them, but the sad thing is they almost all have a large part of their breeding from dairy or Continental breeds, neither of which were meant to outwinter in that worst weather of all for outwintered stock, cold and often freezing rain, of which the Scottish hills get more than their fair share.

As I pen these pages in late 1998 things are not looking good for hill farmers, as sheep prices have plummeted. There seem to be many more sheep than can be consumed in Britain, and for many stupid, mainly bureau-cratic reasons, we are not allowed to export to overseas countries. We have never been a great lamb or mutton-eating country, although personally I could eat cold lamb or mutton 'ad infinitum', but couldn't do the same with beef. What worries me is that until we get the shake-up we are promised with the reform of C.A.P. we may lose all too many young stocksmen who would like to have been able to follow in their fathers' footsteps. So many used to do so, but now they see no future in a shepherd's calling. Of my many shepherd and hill farmer friends I only know of one who has a daugh-ter, yes, a lassie (unheard of in the old days), who wants to follow in her father's footsteps. This is going to be a disaster for the future of the hills of the whole of Great Britain. Those folk were the ones who knew, not only their sheep, but also the land on which the sheep grazed.

How I would love to see a return to smaller units. Oh, I know big units are the only ones that are paying right now because of the subsidy system, but if one could have units of five hundred ewes and twenty hill cows with the emphasis on producing quality lambs and calves, we would be produc-ing quality shepherds at the same time. I know there are some of those around now, but all too few. The big snag is that the size of unit I've sug-gested would need support from some other direction, be it subsidy, part-time employment at slack times or help from the sporting interests like we used to get in the thirties. Anything would be worth it to preserve one of Scot-land's greatest assets, stocksmen. These have also been one of Scotland's greatest exports. I've been lucky to travel to fourteen overseas countries on agricultural business, and in every one there have been either Scottish stocksmen or their descendants.

As I describe what they did in the course of a shepherd's year you will see that they were dedicated men who lived for their sheep and thought of little else.

February

When I was in Sussex in the thirties 'Old Shep' used to talk about this month as 'February fill dyke'. I, callow Scottish youth that I was, thought of 'dykes' as stone walls, not the ditches that are called 'dykes' in England. Little did I think at that time that, after the war, when I was managing a thousand-acre estate in Strathearn, I would be out helping the estate shepherd save sheep in a typical February flood. This had happened when the snow melted on the hills that surrounded the loch that gives the river its name, and coupled with a south-west wind the river broke its banks and flooded Strathearn. As I write in 1998, having come back to Strathearn, it was rather fun and nostalgic for me to come across an account in the local paper of this very event of fifty years ago:

'Two thousand acres of the Strath's agricultural land was under water and then Captain Coutts and the Estate shepherd rowed across the Earn to fifty sheep marooned on an island and drove them into the raging torrent, guiding them at the same time to the bank. Stragglers were beginning to break away and might have been lost had not Captain Coutts jumped fully clad into the water and succeeded in keeping them together'.

The media, even all those fifty years ago, loved to exaggerate, but I certainly do remember getting rid of my heavy ghillie brogues before I swam out to point the leading sheep in the right direction for the shore. I remember little else of the episode, except for the fact that George Menzies, a super stocksman, was, like all shepherds of that era, a non-swimmer. Because of the sort of cottages they had then he probably didn't bath too often either!

That's one of the big problems in the country today, the young shepherds want to start off at the point where we 'oldies' left off—with a car, television, central heating, washing machines, dishwashers etc. etc. With regard to the latter, Sal, my wife, says she doesn't need one as, pointing to me, she says she already has one! High praise.

Sadly some others were not so fortunate as I was. Judy Bowser's shepherd at Auchlyne near Killin was swept away in flood water when endeavouring to rescue a sheep in the raging Dochart river. Scotland lost one of its most forward-looking shepherd managers when Robin Armstrong, manager at Sourhope near Yetholm, was washed away in his Land-rover when the Ale river was in flood. This was not a case where he was actually trying to save sheep but he, like many hundreds of shepherds in the old days, lived in out of the way places that were subject to being blocked in by snow. 1947 was the supreme example of this. The river which originated from the hirsel he shepherded could flood at the drop of a hat if there had been a heavy fall of snow and then a sudden thaw because of a south-west wind. It could not only block the road but also cause massive landslides.

In the old days we had snowfalls the like of which we haven't seen for years. As I've said 1947 was the daddy of them all as far as I was concerned. Some people by then had been feeding their ewes in winter, but all too few. I remember well taking some lovely Norwegian hay (as all Scottish stocks of hay were exhausted) over to Arrivain, just over the Perthshire border in Argyll, to save ewes that the shepherd there said, rightly, were dying of starvation. This hay was like dried grass, lovely looking stuff with a most wonderful 'nose' to it which I think even Oz Clarke, the modern wine buff, would enjoy: it smelt of all those lovely grasses we used to have in our fields in this country pre-war, before the advent of the Common Agricultural Policy and the over-use of nitrogen. Anyway, after taking the ewes this lovely green hay, imagine my feelings when I went back to check, with difficulty I might say because the roads kept getting blocked, to find that they were literally dying rather than eat this manna from heaven.

It was that year I made up my mind to ensure that hill sheep knew about feed other than the herbage that grew on the hill. I reckoned that the right time to start them on other feeds was when they were ewe hoggs. With this in mind they had to be housed, as there was no way they would eat any concentrates if they were left outside and there was a remote chance of them getting any grazing, however scarce. Any amount of flockmasters in-winter their hoggs now, but it was unheard of fifty years ago, and I and others who were experimenting with different types of buildings, feeding troughs (so that the hoggs wouldn't comtaminate the feed or pull all the hay onto the floor) bedding etc. were looked on askance by the 'Aye Beens'. 'It's aye been done this way'—either hoggs were away-wintered or breeked.

But even as early as 1947 there were shepherds who had trained their ewes to feed. The story, probably apocryphal, is told of the shepherd who was 'kirk-greedy' i.e. was a regular attender at his local church because he knew, as I do, how much he had to thank the Almighty for—'all things bright and beautiful, all creatures great and small'. In the middle of the 1947 storm, he set out for church as usual, attended by his dogs, which was often the case then as they would lie contentedly in the church porch. As the snow was deep his legs were swathed in bits of hessian sack held in place by binder twine, unlike today when they would be replaced by those super snow-leggings that everyone using the hills in winter wears. Imagine his amazement when he gets to the door to be greeted by the minister, who had been hoping no one would turn up, with: 'Well, Geordie, as you are the only member of the congregation to turn up on this horrendous day, we'll cancel the service'. But Geordie would have none of this and replies, 'Meenister, when I tend my flock in bad weather and only one turns up she aye gets a feed'. So the minister, inwardly blazing, gave Geordie the lot: two lengthy readings, equally long prayers, a sermon that wound up with 'finally' (which means at least ten more minutes), and then went to the door to shake Geordie's hand, thinking 'that'll fix him'. When Geordie came forward the minister said. 'I hope you enjoyed the service, Geordie'. To which he replied. 'When one sheep comes to the trough I gie her a handful of feed, not the whole bloody bag'.

Snow can be a shepherd's worst enemy, or was in the old days when we had harder winters and the in-wintering of the ewe stock was unheard of. February always used to be a snowy month in the Highlands, although in the West it could be quite balmy, yet as I write in 1998 we have had the warmest February since records began. It was not always thus, and in 1953 there were massive losses because of a fierce snow storm that lasted all too long. The snag is that sheep naturally turn their backs to a storm and are then gently propelled by the wind to the nearest shelter, which on open hills is all too often a deep burn. The sheep stand in there and the snow is blown off the land on the windward side until the gully is level. The sheep can end up smothered in many feet of snow, and as I know to my cost it can take an awful lot of shovelling before one gets down to the beleaguered beasties. However there are some amazing stories of sheep living for weeks in those ice igloos by, believe it or not, eating each other's wool.

Pat tells a story that he was told by an old shepherd when he was starting shepherding, of a big snow storm in 1906. This was in the days when people ate mutton instead of lamb, and many hirsels which are now stocked with ewes carried stocks of three-year-old wethers. One such was Blairmore in the mouth of Glenartney which had a stock of six hundred wethers. The snowstorm was sudden and severe. There were no weather forecasts on the T.V. in those days—there was no radio, far less T.V. in those days—and although shepherds were extremely good at foretelling the weather they couldn't tell what the severity of a storm would be. On this occasion they got caught out, and it was with great difficulty they managed to get all but thirty-nine of their sheep gathered 'inbye'. For a whole month, with dogs sniffing, and plunging poles into snowdrifts, they hunted for those missing wethers but to no avail. After five weeks the thaw came and the wethers were found in a deep burn where they had barely three hundred yards in which to move up and down. They had rumped the heather which overhung the burn down to the roots and then started on their own wool. They were extremely weak, but amazingly only one died. The sheep were as hardy as the shepherds in these days!

Then in 1940 when Pat was home on leave from the R.A.F. he had to help his father get a cut of ewes down from Ben Vorlich where they had been stranded by a sudden storm. The rough track from the head of the glen out to the Ben was blocked with drifts, and they both knew that unless they could make some sort of a track the ewes would never come out. What they did was cut a twelve foot long spruce tree about eighteen inches in diameter and yoked two ponies to it, one to each end. The pole pulled between them flattened a path in the snow which was about a foot deep except where it was drifted. Pat's father had wisely kept an old favourite of a ewe long after she should have been cast, and she set off ahead of the rest down the track. Although there were times when she had a job getting through some of the deeper bits, she never stopped until she got back to Auchinner at the head of Glenartney. A leader is essential in all walks of life, be it politics, the Church, you name it, but never more than in a flock of sheep. Hence the use in Eastern countries of the old 'bell wether', which was a wether with a bell hung round his neck. The bell wether not only told the shepherd where his flock was grazing, but was the leader when the shepherd wanted to move the flock. In the East the sheep follow the shepherd, they are not driven as we do in the West.

Pat's stories about the famous 1947 storm are horrendous. Although the whole country suffered that year, and touch wood I hope won't have to suffer in the same way again, some shepherds had it worse than others. In Glenartney, for instance, the drifts were so deep that when the one hundred and ten prisoners of war were sent out to work from the Prisoner of War Camp in Comrie, they hung their jackets on the top of the telegraph poles! One of the main road bridges was washed away in the floods afterwards, and it was a year before it was replaced. Coal stocks ran out and the lady who owned the estate authorised the shooting lodge stock to be used as there was no coal coming into Comrie station. As for supplies in those days, most homes had flour and oatmeal enough for the winter, and lean white hares and venison helped out. The deer officially could only be killed before the fifteenth of February, the end of the hind shooting season, but many starving beasts had to be humanely put down long after that date. The hardy Glenartney Highland ponies, under Peter MacIntyre, were the lifeline of the Glen in that infamous year, one that those of us who had to work through it would wish to forget.

For Pat it was a nightmare. He managed to get his ewes off the hill and was able to get them to take a bite of hay, as he had them enclosed, unlike the ewes at Arrivain which were on an open hill and refused to eat, as mentioned earlier in the chapter. The real disaster for him was when they made their minds up to get back to their hefts, but were so weak they kept falling in the burns. He lost seventy out of his four hundred, and many other hill farms had huge losses. Lambing too was terrible in that year, as ewes were so lean they had little or no milk, and Pat only marked (of that later) one hundred and ten out of his four hundred ewes. February was a disaster in 1947.

The weight of snow never ceases to amaze me. In the last century landlords in the Highlands found this out when they tried to fence their sheep on their own ground. Had they been shepherded properly by hefting, as I've explained in the last chapter, a huge expense could have been saved. I've seen the remnants of their march (boundary) fences in Badenoch in Upper Speyside, and in West Perthshire and Argyll, where all that is left are the metal straining posts. These have only remained because they were sunk into rocks and bedded in with lead. As the lead would need to be heated so that it could be poured round each post, and as many of those strainers were between two thousand to three thousand feet above sea level, I shudder to think what the cost was, even in those far-off days. Every one I've seen of those march fences has been flattened by snow. The snow comes down vertically but as it thaws it moves and literally takes all before it. What a pity the likes of the Earl of Breadalbane didn't 'Ride the Marches' like the Borderers do to see what a fantastic waste of money was being incurred.

Today a lot of old-time shepherds would take a dim view of the modern idea of fencing, where untreated green stobs (posts) are used to sustain an electric wire or two compared with the seven wire (six plain and one barb) fences of the old days. These were fastened to weathered larch stobs and strained by posts that were sunk four feet in the ground with a 'breest' (breast) stone in front and a 'heelstane' behind at the bottom of the pit. This meant one could really tighten the wires as they altered with extremes of temperature.

But sadly all too many hill farms don't have enclosed land, so that fencing wouldn't be a regular job for shepherds on those vast Highland holdings. All the same, most hill farmers and their shepherds like to have some 'in bye' land, which is really indispensable for holding sheep for all the different operations one has to perform, like marking lambs, clipping, dipping, preparation for sales etc., etc. But believe me, nothing, but nothing, can find a way through a fence more easily than an old hill ewe who wants to get back to her 'bit'! and it's amazing how much maintenance a fence requires.

In the old days wool was what the Blackfaced breed was famous for. There always seemed to be a war going on, and in the past that was when wool was most wanted for clothing, blankets, uniforms, etc. Judging by the ex-army First World War kilts I wore as a schoolboy, and the ex-army blankets I have slept in, both as prickly as porcupines, they contained wool from Blackfaced fleeces. The snag about breeding for wool was that the ewe grew it everywhere, including all around her udder, and if one wanted the lamb to get a decent suck one had to turn the ewe upside-down on her backside and 'udder-luck' her, i.e. pluck the wool off the udder, a long and painstaking task. I don't know how you spell it, but before the last war it was common practice to gather the flock or hirsel or heft, to liver-fluke-dose and 'udder-luck' the ewes.

With the demand for meat after the war, and remember it was still rationed in the early fifties, flockmasters started to think about the meat potential of their flocks. The Cheviots had always been famous for being extra good for meat production in the spring of the year. But it was not until a few years after the last war that the majority of Blackfaced flockmasters realised that if they bred sheep with shorter coats, 'bare coated' they called them, that they would have (a) a milkier ewe and (b) an earlier maturing lamb. Back in the late forties and early fifties, thanks to my boss and mentor in stock breeding, Duncan Stewart, I was in the van of those who used 'bare coated' tups and got a lot of stick from the old-established tup breeders for voicing my views on 'Farm Forum', a weekly broadcast of which I was part. Strangely enough all those very same tup breeders went in for what were called the 'Newton Stewart' type of tup within the next few years. As that great dog handler and tup breeder Jimmy Wilson once said to me, 'Ben, you're no doing any guid till they're all agin' ye'.

When Pat and I started thinking about this book and the differences between shepherding in the old days and modern times we thought the greatest change was embodied in that famous couplet 'What is this life so full of care, there is no time to stand and stare'. We reckoned that the times we had sat down on the hill just spying with our 'glass' (telescope) had been more than rewarding. Until I couldn't go to the hill any more because of 'anno domini' I had a lovely lightweight telescope that belonged to Findlay MacIntosh, the head stalker on the Ardverikie Estate on which I was a tenant farmer, and on which estate they later filmed the Oscar-nominated 'Mrs Brown'. In the words of one of my bosses, a famous London business-man, 'There's no secrets on the hill, Ben'. He then recounted to me how he had once witnessed a love affair between two very famous people. Had the story been told to today's press it would have been worth a fortune but (a) he was a gentleman and (b) he wouldn't have needed the money anyway.

Pat also told a story about a love affair, but between four-legged, not two-legged, lovers. He was out on the hill in late February, and as was usual in the old days when one wanted to take a breather he sat down and took out his 'glass' (no, sadly in those days it wasn't one in which to pour a much-needed dram). When Pat started spying, what did he see but two dog foxes chasing a vixen close to a well-known earth half-way up Ben Vorlich. When he got back to Auchinner, the centre of operations in Glenartney, he told the assembled company, shepherds, keepers, ghillies et al., 'there'll be cubs in the Ben Vorlich den in the first week in June'. Pat, like me, is known as 'T.T.M.' (Talks Too Much)—probably why we get on so well and are writing this book! Anyway he was laughed to scorn, as vixens usually cub April to May. Pat went out in the first week in June, and sure enough there were the vixen and cubs in the Ben Vorlich earth.

As I pen this chapter I am in my wee office which has a wonderful view of the beginning of the Grampians to the north, and a northern view is always the best. I can see smoke, obviously fanned by an east wind as the month is March, so they will be burning heather, an essential task to keep the herbage on a hill fit for sheep and grouse. In February, if the shepherd

My old boss and friend, Pat MacNab, out on the hills of Glenartney, with Ben Vorlich and the Stuich in the background.

got on with the keeper, he would help him make those huge brooms of birch to beat out fires that were going in the wrong direction. But the burning itself is a March or early April job, before the grouse nest, and by law the latest date for doing it is the fifteenth of April, unless one is burning above four hundred and fifty metres.

March

A song that was popular in the days when I listened to the dance bands of the thirties—Jack Hylton, Roy Fox, Harry Roy, Carol Gibbons et al—went: 'March winds and April showers make way for sweet May flowers'. (No wonder I couldn't pass my vet. exams when I spent so much time listening to that rubbish!) In those days there certainly were March winds, and they came from the east. I know as an oldie one always think things have changed, but I'm certain the weather pattern is altering as we don't get the severe winters we used to get, and we don't get the harsh east winds for days on end.

The arable farmers always liked those winds because they would dry up the ground to let them start to sow their grain. The keepers liked them because they could make a real job of their 'muirburn'. That is the name given to the job of burning heather, and on any well run estate it should be performed by keepers and shepherds working together. But sadly from my own experience this doesn't always happen, as the former are thinking of their grouse and the latter of their precious ewes. The object should be the same for both: to burn off the old, often foot-high, wooden heather so that in time it will sprout from the roots, giving a nutritious bite of new growth for grouse and ewes alike. The secret is to burn it in patches, like a patchwork quilt, hence the brooms have to be kept nearby to put out the fire if it gets out of hand. Sadly, some shepherds I have known seemed to think that everything should be burnt, as if this is done one gets a flush of (quite useless and short-lived) green weeds after the first warm rain. As mentioned in the last chapter, one is allowed to muirburn until 15 April when the grouse will be thinking of nesting. One is allowed go on later if one is only burning on the 'high tops'. A well-managed hill farm or estate will have some longish heather, not so long that you can hardly walk through it, but long enough to give shelter for grouse and other birds and sheep; some younger heather succulent enough for sheep, deer and grouse to eat; and the really young growth especially enjoyed by all three.

I remember well an incident on an estate where I was a ponyman pre-war. This estate had a really well-managed heather-burning policy so that even the oldest block of heather wasn't impassable. We were picking up dead grouse after a drive, and one of the pickers-up who would be getting an extra ten shillings (fifty pence) per day for his quite useless cross collie-Labrador was trying to get the dog to pick up a grouse that I could see lying in a patch of medium-sized heather. The dog had been mucking about for at least ten minutes and the order had been given by the head keeper to move on to the next drive, so I made a move to retrieve the bird. At this 'Duncan the Birach' (God knows how he came by the name) shouted: 'Gie the dog a chance, the bloody keeper should burn his heather'. The dog had had ten minutes and the heather was perfect!—but I knew that Duncan would badly need that ten shillings, as times were hard in the thirties.

Like many a job carried out by craftsmen, and shepherds and keepers were just that, there was and is a right and a wrong way of burning heather. I got great pleasure, when I was factoring an estate in the north, in giving a young keeper a real bollocking for lighting a fire with the wind behind him. When this is done it is just like those forest fires one sees on T.V. in Australia or Brazil, where the flames leap from treetop to treetop. With heather it does the same, the flames catching only the tops of the plants and not burning down to the roots which they do when burning against the wind. Not only that, the fires are much more easily extinguished when burnt against the wind. In the case I'm quoting the lad's fire got completely out of control and (a) burnt a huge area and (b) necessitated me asking a whole gang of neighbours to help dowse the flames. However I hear the said lad is now a first-class head keeper, who I'm sure will enjoy telling his juniors how to 'muirburn'.

It's sad how our hill management has deteriorated over the years, and I suppose it is all to do with us wanting a higher standard of living. Now landowners and hill farmers can't afford the labour which was essential for keeping cattle on the hill. These cattle controlled the molinia and nardus grasses and left their manure, but the cattle not much fatter, only six months older. And labour was needed to look after and properly herd a five hundred ewe hirsel so that the sheep didn't overgraze the bottoms of the hills and leave the tops ungrazed as one sees all too often today. And labour was needed to control the deer stocks that in all too many areas have got out of hand. When one considers how few mountain hares, the white ones, one sees today, and the grouse numbers compared with the numbers in the thirties, it's sad, sad.

One of the March jobs for shepherds used to be to help the keepers with their hare drives. It's amazing to think that as many as a thousand hares would be killed in one day in Glenartney, and when you think that five hares will eat as much as a ewe you can appreciate how well the available feed was managed in those days. And Glenartney wasn't the only estate and hill farm that was well managed, the majority were, whereas sadly now for all too many reasons it's the minority that are well run. The biggest reason for poor management, which I've repeatedly said and will say again, is that the headage subsidy is based on the ewe stock instead of being a labour-related one.

My introduction to shooting white hares, called 'the hare hunt' for some unknown reason, despite the fact that no dogs were involved, was being put in charge of three ponies each of which had to carry sixty hares. The ponies had deer saddles, and we would cut a hole in the hare's skin on the hind leg above the hock and thread the deer saddle strap, that was there for keeping a stag on the saddle, through this hole. When I graduated to being one of the guns I was sent out to the top of the line. I was frightfully conceited at being given this spot, as it is the one to which the hares always go, but I was soon deflated when I started to pick up and carry my hares down to the ponies, as they were damned heavy, and my heart went out to the ponies having to carry sixty of them!

I remember taking the famous plastic surgeon Sir Archibald McIndoe, who had come north to shoot geese with me, out to shoot white hares. By the end of the shoot he reckoned a surgeon's life was not a good training ground for a day on a snowy hill! 'Archie' gave me my new nose after the old one was shot away by a bit of German shrapnel in the Tobruk garrison. I owed him a lot, and was sad that the geese weren't flighting properly when he came to stay with me back in the late forties. But he did pot a white hare or two, and afterwards enjoyed regaling his posh friends in the south about the rigours of white hare shooting compared to the driven pheasant shoots that they attended.

The geese that I had invited Archie to come to shoot used to come in from the saltings on the coast in the mornings to graze in Strathearn during the day and fly back at nightfall. Now we have them in the Strath the whole winter, and they have three lochs in which they can drink and preen themselves daily. The lochs are Dupplin, Abercairney and Carsbreck. The last-named is the one on which the great curling bonspiel was held before the war. Now, if we ever had the thickness of ice needed for the event, the loch would be far too small to hold it, so popular has the sport become.

The mention of geese in the Coutts family always brings out snide remarks about the old man's ability to pluck a goose. One Christmas time Sal remarked: 'Why do we always have to have turkey? How about a goose for a change?' Whereupon yours truly replied: 'There's a Christmas Sale of turkeys, geese, cockerels etc. in MacDonald Fraser's Mart in Perth, I'll go and buy one.' I duly went in and bought a huge gander (and was to learn later that his size must have been due to his age). When I got him home and tried to 'thraw' (wring) his neck, the usual swift way of despatching a fowl, I was completely beat. Eventually, after ringing up a pal, I found out how to do it, by a method which was very easy and an immediate and painless death to the goose. I then went into the house and said to Sal: 'I'm out in the byre plucking the goose if you want me'. To which she replied: 'I'll skin it, which is much easier'. Conceited as always and thinking my ability to pluck a goose was being called into question I said: 'Don't be silly, you can't roast it properly if it's not plucked'. Three hours later Sal popped her head into the byre to find an exasperated husband, covered in goose down, using words that no elder of the Church of Scotland should know, far less use, and using a pair of sheep shears to cut off the toughest of the feathers. The story has rightly become a family joke about Dad not listening to Mum etc., etc., but how was Dad to know he had bought the Methuselah of all Methuselahs of a goose! This story has nothing to do with a shepherd's year, except that it shows the author knows how to use a pair of hand shears. But to anyone given a goose I have no hesitation in saying: 'Skin it!'

I talked about one sort of burning in March, i.e. the muirburn: but on grassy hills there could be another which, unlike heather burning, did no good at all, and that was the east wind burning off the grass. Donald MacPherson who, like Pat MacNab, has been feeding me with information for this book, recalls that in the '47 winter when the rest of the country was feet deep in snow, at the head of Loch Fyne where he was shepherding they hadn't an inch of it. What they did have was an icy wind from the east, lasting from November until March, that killed the grazing and also too many of his ewes! The only consolation was that they were able to curl on their outdoor curling rink for five months. Loch Fyne is a sea loch, so we're talking about conditions at sea level. What differences shepherds can face in this small island of ours because of climate! Then Donald talked of the season of 1951, when his lambing percentage was a mere forty-nine per cent (even in the fifties, which was before we hand-fed our hill ewes, a normal lambing would be round about eighty per cent). In over sixty years of shepherding, for which Donald got a well deserved B.E.M., 1951 was the only year he witnessed ewes which were so lean they were dropping their lambs as they walked on to try to find another bite. Usually, as any reader will know, all animals (including the human variety) lie down to have their young.

I will always remember an occasion when I was Agricultural Adviser to the T.V. show *Strathblair*, and we were shooting a scene about the spring dipping. We wanted to use yeld ewes, as all too often the filming shoots need retakes or one is asked to hold a sheep for longer in the dipper than would be good for a ewe heavily in lamb. In the fank on the way to the dipper the sheep farmer and I had pulled out the odd in-lamb ewe that had accidentally got in with the yeld ones, and one of these ewes was starting to lamb. We had to put them in a side bucht out of sight of the camera. Before every shot the familiar clapper-board is shown to camera with 'Shot Five Take One' or whatever and then the Director says, 'Quiet'. Just as the Director, a lady, said this the old ewe in the bucht let out a great grunt, whereupon the Director, in a stentorian voice, exclaimed, 'I said quiet!' Yet again the old ewe let out a grunt. I and my team of shepherds who were helping me, and what a grand bunch they were, were standing out of shot but just over a stone wall from the old ewe. One, I know not who, said: 'You'd be gruntin' too, lassie, if you were doing what the old ewe's doing'. Yes, usually the lambs don't slip out they are forced out.

The average death rate in the extensive West Highland sheep farms, known as 'black loss', was ten per cent, again this was before the advent of feeding, in-wintering etc. It always amazed me in the many years that I managed those sort of units that we never found half of the carcasses for that ten per cent loss. Did they get washed away in those awful spates that the Highlands are subject to? Were they eaten by foxes or hoodie crows? If so where were the bones? Did they get into peat bogs? I don't know, but one of my bosses, the late Lord Glenkinglas (Michael Noble, Secretary of State for Scotland when I managed for him), was brilliant at knowing the percentage of black loss he would have on each hirsel. But even he was beat when Donald told him that he was about to have a death rate of forty per cent on his hirsel in 1951. In that year it wasn't a case of where did the dead sheep go, they sadly were to be seen dead all over the hill, and I know from personal experience what a rotten job it is to bury dead ewes that you have looked after, and in many cases knew as characters. Luckily in those days we could all use a spade, but even more luckily nowadays we've learnt that feeding at the right time can obviate a lot of the infamous black loss.

When the hoggs came back from their wintering it was either the end of March or beginning of April. The winterers always wanted them away as early as possible, as the fences on most of their farms were diabolical and the hoggs had the run of the place, which included the fields of young grass. In those days most small farmers in areas that were used by us hill farmers for wintering their hoggs were still using what was called the 'seven course shift', i.e. three years crop and four of grass. This meant that a field each year would be sown out as new grass which would be made into hay in its first year. It only needs a frost and thaw alternating each night to ruin a young grass field if the hoggs have access to it, as they can pull the grass out by the roots. We hill people on the other hand who had probably had a March wind were thinking of our precious ewe stock and wanted to delay the return of the hoggs for as long as possible.

When they came back they had to be dipped, horn-branded and keeled for their respective hirsels. Tick was one of the biggest problems in the west as they carried the dreaded 'louping ill', which was a killer, so the hoggs had to be dipped immediately on their return. Michael Noble told me a story against himself about ticks. Donald had pushed up his lambing percentage by drawing out his lean ewes and putting them in the 'Policy Parks' around the big hoose, Ardkinglas, where they got some much better grazing, at sea level, than up on their own hirsel. Michael managed to get a good farm, that had been tenanted, back into his own hands. He thought to himself, 'if Donald could improve his lambing percentage by using better land, I'll bring in the furthest-out hirsel I own and give them a month pre-lambing on this

An old boiler of the kind which used to stand beside every dipper in the old days. The dip came in blocks and had to be melted before use with boiling water from the boiler.

good arable land'. What happened? They started dying like flies, and why? Because they had no immunity to ticks. Ticks couldn't survive on that far away hirsel which was well over the one thousand five hundred foot mark. Donald recounts that for him the only funny part of this sad story was seeing the research vets who were called in (and which research team or college wouldn't jump to the Secretary of State for Scotland's request, or was it an order?) to find out the cause of the death. What made him laugh was to see those high-powered guys (yes, and dolls) dragging a blanket over the field to which the ticks became attached. When they got enough ticks gathered they took them off to their laboratory, I suppose to find out to which species they belonged. But Michael never tried that experiment again.

Any reader of this book who is a townee, if I have any such, may wonder why sheep have coloured markings on different parts of their body e.g. behind the head, on the shoulder, the tail or head etc. These denote to which hirsel they belong. The hoggs are marked, 'keeled' as it is called, when they come back from their wintering. There are three forms of identification on Blackfaced ewes: lug marking, which I'll talk about in the June chapter, and keeling and horn branding which is done when the ewe hoggs come back from their wintering.

The 'keeling' was done as the sheep emerged from its 'cold bath' in the dipper, and was looked on as rather a cushy job. As a result it was taken on by the oldest or laziest member of the squad (which was me if I was there). One used a bit of a broom handle with something on the end that resembled a large sponge or a modern microphone (the like of which one sees being pushed into people's faces during those all too frequent interviews with politicians, footballers etc.). The sponge bit was actually made from hessian. All our sacks were hessian, and they had so many uses after they were emptied of their original contents, unlike the polythene ones we get today, which one has a job to destroy, far less re-use.

The horn branding was done by the head shepherd or the farmer if present. On the near horn was branded the farm brand, for instance my brand when I farmed Gaskbeg in upper Speyside was GB. On the off horn was branded the ewe's year of birth, e.g. '8' if born in 1998, and as all hill ewes are cast at five or six years old there is no need for double numbers.

The only snag with horn branding in the West is that, because the high rainfall leaches the calcium out of the ground, the horns are very brittle. Unless one wanted to be like the housemaid who broke a precious plate and when berated by her employer said: 'It came away in me hand, Ma'am', one couldn't grab an Argyll ewe by the horn as you could with a ewe in, say, the

Angus glens. I once saw a sight that I'll never forget, it was a day I was gathering sheep on Arrivain which lies just West of Tyndrum and has a high rainfall. There was a single ewe being chased down the hill to join the main bunch, and she was not travelling normally but kept leaping in the air off all four legs so that she resembled a boulder coming down a hillside. On one of the occasions when her four feet hit the ground her two horns shot into the air! So you can see why we didn't dare handle the Argyll ewes by their horns, though despite this I saw all too many ewes with but a single horn. Although I was usually told they'd been knocked off in some of those old stone fanks we used, I sometimes 'had my doots'.

As I pen the end of the March chapter it's actually the first week of April and it's snowing. I'm glad, at my age, to be, thanks to the central heating which was unheard of forty years ago in farm houses and cottages, snug as a bug in a rug. I'm looking out on a sturdy old brazier that I used for branding the Ben Challum hoggs and Fordie Highland cattle all those fifty years ago, and remembering many a cold snowy day when the hoggs came back and we had to get on with the job as we hadn't enough holding parks. Nowadays most shepherds will be doing the job under cover in one of those huge sheds that have now been erected on most hill farms. My girls called the brazier 'Dad's brassiere'—but I think the former would give more welcome heat than the latter on some of those cold east wind days that we used to get!

April

'I doot she'll no hear the "coo-coo" [cuckoo]', was a favourite saying of my shepherd at Gaskbeg when we would come across a weak lean ewe in wintertime. In the Highlands, the shepherds used to look forward to the return of the birds that wintered away but summered in the hills. I still love the return of the whaup (the curlew) with its haunting cry heralding the coming of spring when everything comes to life again and animals give birth. And then there were the oyster catchers with their black and white colouring, striding around and calling stridently for all the world like Church of Scotland ministers of the old school (my father was one but not a strident one). Then the lovely lapwings, the peewits. The shepherds' name for them was the 'teuchets', and the shepherds always reckoned it would be just when their lambing started in April that they would get the 'teuchet storm'. Now as I write in 1998 we are getting it after a mild February and March.

Sadly the numbers of all birds that nest on the ground are decreasing and it always annoys me that the Royal Society for the Protection of Birds want to give more protection to raptors than they do to other species. This was demonstrated recently when a trial was done to see the number of hen harriers that a moor could carry. The trial was carried out near Lockerbie, and when it was proven that there were too many hen harriers, instead of reducing their numbers the R.S.P.B. wanted some pairs sent to another moor. But if you think the author is agin all raptors you'd be terribly wrong as I've spent hours lying in the heather watching eagles, hen harriers, ravens etc. all with their different and glorious use of the thermal air currents. Watching a pair of hen harriers quartering a grouse moor and seeing the number of ground-nesting birds they collect it reminds me of the wife's hoover (the noise of which annoys me as much as the sight of the hen harriers hoovering a moor). But how I love their flight. And also that of the ravens, which must have the best eyesight of all raptors. They will be at the site of the gralloch of a stag within minutes of the stalker and the rifle (i.e. the gent who shot the beast) and the ghillie having left the spot. And ditto if they see a weakly new-born lamb with its umbilical cord still red—ravens appear from nowhere and tear the stomach out of the lamb, and then fight over their spoils, yes, even in mid-air. 'Nature in the raw is seldom mild' as the old saying goes: and this is what sadly so many townees who come to the country don't appreciate.

April is the busiest month of the year for shepherds, but the reason I started this chapter as I did is to try to make readers realise that shepherds love their surroundings and the birds that inhabit it, though some of them don't help him at his job. So the month of April can start for them with the hill birds returning and with high hopes of a good lambing ahead, but can finish with a disaster due to many reasons. The chief of these is inclement weather, which modern shepherds on the majority of hill farms have been able to combat by lambing inside, using inbye parks etc.

But let's look at a hill shepherd's April forty to fifty years ago. In the better areas of our hills the tups will go out on 20 November, which means that the lambing will start on 19 April. On the high, almost ranch-like Highland estates, however, the tups could be kept inbye (in some cases in byres and stables, so keen are some tups to get on with the job) until 1 December, which meant lambing would start on 30 April. The shepherd's year depended on a good lambing, and it's amazing how many lambs could be saved by a good shepherd compared with an idle one. How times have changed: until as recently as twenty years ago shepherds would have to walk miles before they got to their lambing ewes. Both Pat and Donald had two miles plus to do, and then they did a good twelve hour stint at the lambing. They then had to walk home their miles, probably with two or three twin lambs in the lambing bag which they all carried. It's amazing how heavy a lamb or two can be, even without having done a full day's work. The reason that hill shepherds would be taking home lambs is that on our wild open hills, if a ewe makes a good job of rearing a single lamb it's all you can expect of her, whereas on an arable farm they want twins and triplets. It's all a matter of feed and environment. It's amazing to think that just a few years ago there was a thriving trade for those motherless twin lambs which could make £6-£10 at ten days old, whereas now, since the drop in the export market, yearling hoggs are only making £20-£30.

So the hill shepherd is on his hirsel and is quietly going through his ewes to see what has lambed or what is in trouble lambing. The first thing he wants is a quiet dog, especially if he is to catch a ewe. I know the dog trials, quite rightly, don't want dogs that grip, but one that wears a ewe to you gently and then grips it by the wool on the neck, while doing no harm to the ewe, can be more than useful. If you don't catch that ewe out on that brae face and she heads off down the hill, as she is bound to do, probably with a lamb half-hanging out of her, she will (a) be all hell to catch next time, and (b) if her lamb is dead she will be extremely difficult when one tries to set another lamb on to her. Although many things have changed in a shepherd's year in the last fifty years, one thing hasn't, and that is that the only way to get a ewe that has lost her lamb to accept another is to skin the dead lamb and put the skin on the lamb that one wishes the ewe to rear. I remember when my girls were wee and on the odd occasions I had to undress them I said, 'now we'll skin the lamb' as I pulled their clothes off from backside to head, because that's what one does with a dead lamb's skin. Starting at the rear end leaving the hind legs and tail with the dead carcase, it's easy to skin a lamb. One leaves two holes to slip the fore legs through, ditto the head, so when one puts the skin over the living lamb all one has to do is to make insertions for the hind legs depending how big the living lamb might be. I never cease to wonder at the sense of smell that all animals have compared with us mere humans: not only does the shepherd put on the skin of the ewe's own lamb, but he'll have to rub the live lamb's head and tail with the dead lamb's skin to make sure the ewe thinks it's hers.

One of the greatest assets that a shepherd could have in the old days was a wife who was interested in his job and wanted to help him at lambing time. They would have a 'house cow' which she would milk. There would be one of those famous old fashioned black 'Carron' ranges (which ate coal), beside which she would have a 'hay box', literally a box with hay in it, the lovely meadow sort we never see today, in which orphan lambs were deposited. These were bottle-fed with the cow's milk diluted and with sugar added. But of course the first milk any animal can get, the colostrum, is the one that cleans out the system and gets all animals going. I always remember my Dad, a Church of Scotland minister who loved all things to do with the land, being told by an old shepherd in Dumfriesshire that if a lamb had 'ae sook' it would outlive a human in wintry conditions. The same shepherd when asked by a friend of father's what he thought about Dad's sermon that Sunday said, 'No bad, but it tak's a man to herd the Merrick.' The Merrick being the highest hill in the south west.

When a ewe had a dead lamb it could be as much as half a mile from the nearest parrock or fank, and one had to drag the lamb there by a bit of binder twine so that the ewe would follow it. Nowadays, lambing inside, one only has a few yards to move the ewe so that one can 'set on' a twin, what a time-saver. Some canny ewes could be tied to a sturdy bit of heather while one 'set on' the lamb, but canny hill ewes were few and far between fifty years ago when it was a case of the survival of the fittest. Nowadays the hill ewes are so used to being in-wintered or at least in inbye fields that they will be more amenable, but sadly probably never see the high tops where the heather grows.

In the old days in the Highlands there were the 'shielings' of which we have all heard. These were built of stone, and with a bit of sheep netting or larch rails could be made into useful twinning parrocks. These shielings were well out at the top of the glens in the Highlands. In the days when cattle, not sheep, grazed the Highland hills the cattle were wintered inside, often in part of the human dwelling house, and in the summer were sent out to the top of the glens to be herded by a young member of the family who had to milk the cows and make butter out of the cream to help out the family's winter rations. This meant they had to have an enclosure in which they could milk the cows, hence the building of the shielings.

I am writing about a shepherd's year and the way of life fifty years ago, but it never ceases to amaze me how the Highlanders of even earlier times survived, never mind made the odd bob or two. Yet, come to think of it, what would they spend money on, as they clothed themselves in their own woollen materials, they made their own butter, they bled their cattle to make their black puddings and the odd beast would die now and again. Although they didn't have deep freezes they did have some ways of conserving food, although in the eighteenth century it was before the days of the brine tub.

In those far-off days, just as fifty years ago, how much the men depended on the womenfolk for physical help in running the unit, be it croft, hill farm, shepherding or any set up to do with the land. Now, with the so called 'equality of the sexes', shepherds' wives want their own jobs, they are not willing to help their husbands with sickly or orphan lambs and want to do their own thing. Who are the 'Three Musketeers', Pat, Donald and I, to judge them, as we all had wives who helped us at this essential and most exacting time of the year. Although all the modern inwintering of the ewes, inoculations, injections, scientific knowledge, four-wheeled motorbikes etc., etc., have made things so much easier for the modern shepherd, I wonder if he has that hot meal ready for him that we looked forward to after our fourteen to eighteen hour stint, and which was waiting for us when we wearily sank into the chair. Was the 'dogs' meat' (as we called the dogs' supper in those days, though it had no meat content) ready for those marvellous servants?

Fifty years ago the dogs would have run fifty or sixty miles on a day like that—the lambing shepherd will have done twelve miles plus and a dog does at least four times what he does. The awful thing was that then we didn't realise what a balanced diet was, and all too many excellent sheep dogs were fed either porridge and skimmed milk or flaked maize and skimmed milk, and the only time they got any protein was at the lambing when they ate the ewes' afterbirth. So keen were they to do this that I have seen some of the best dogs I know, who would normally obey every command or whistle from their master, stop to scoff an afterbirth before moving on to gather the ewes and lambs. Nowadays there are so many specialised feeds for dogs I fear someone must be making some money out of the business.

All I do know is that the dogs we had fifty years ago, for all their malnutrition, lasted until they were ten or twelve years old and could really shift a bulk of sheep, which all too few can do today, but only if they avoided getting the dreaded distemper. I can't remember when distemper was first 'sorted out' by the veterinary profession, but it was a killer for all too many years. Donald remembers that on one large Highland estate in the thirties they lost thirty dogs. I remember well when I was gathering sheep on Arrivain with Geordie Menzies, who later came to work with me at Gaskbeg and always had super dogs. He was gathering the top of Ben Dhu and I the bottom when I heard him shout, which was unusual for him, as like all good handlers he usually only whistled. When I looked up I was aghast to see his best bitch 'Fly' hurtling down through the rocks of the near sheer face of Ben Dhu which one can see on the left hand side of Glen Lochy. That was the end of the gathering that day, and the only time I saw Geordie, a survivor of the horrors of the first war, in tears as he cradled 'Fly' in his arms. The local vet pronounced she had had a distemper fit.

A happier story of Geordie was when he was with me at Gaskbeg in the fifties and he went, as did all the inhabitants of Lagganbridge, to see the first showing of T.V. in the Village Hall. The whole district turned out to look at this small square black-and-white T.V. set showing Frank Sinatra singing. On the way home from the hall my youngest son Donald, who was a great chum of old Geordie's, said to him, 'What did you think of that, Geordie?' To which the reply was, 'Just a big star in a wee picture'. In later life Donald took after the side of my character that had enjoyed broadcasting and T.V. appearances, and went into the world of T.V. himself. The first company he set up was called 'A Big Star in a Wee Picture'. I wonder why?

Then of course in April we had the dreaded fox and hoodie crow menace. They would be rearing young then, and food is a scarce commodity at that time of year especially if we'd had a bad winter. It amazes me how all too many people still think of foxes as if they were all cuddly toys. They have never seen the carnage a fox can commit in a hen house as I have, where but one hen is eaten and sixteen others are killed just for fun. As for the remaining eight, they never laid another egg that year and it was hell and all to get them inside the henhouse at night after their experience.

Pat tells of the morning he went out in Lanarkshire and found eight dead lambs, and his neighbour just over the March dyke had seven, so that single fox despatched fifteen in one night and only one eaten. Every year there are tales of lambs being killed by foxes, but they are very clever as they never kill near their dens. Just as the 'travelling folk' of old never poached near their resting places! I remember Wattie Burton at Cononish, Tyndrum, where they are now hoping to find gold, being an expert at knowing where the vixen would have her den if you told him where the lambs were being killed. Back in the late forties I, as a callow youth, told him that we were losing lambs on the Kirkton face above Crianlarich. Putting his bonnet on the back of his head and pushing his nose up with his hand (a favourite gesture of his when he was laying down the law), he pronounced: 'She'll be in the Tol Dhu'. The Tol Dhu was on the back of Ben Challum, a good two hours march from the Kirkton face, and I in my innocence questioned his judgement. So he told me to go there with the squad the following morning. Sure enough, she was there and the earth was surrounded with all too many lamb bones. But I had to admire any animal who would go so far to bring back food for her young when there were lambs much nearer her den, but like the travelling folk she wouldn't 'dirty her own doorstep' as the saying goes.

This is no place to go into the pros and cons of fox hunting, but in my experience the most humane way of dealing with hill foxes was the old gin trap. Before you explode with rage, reader, let me explain how it was laid. First, find a loch with a wee island near the shore, build a narrow causeway to it and set the trap on it, having first put the bait pinned down on the island. If the trap catches a fox he is drowned within seconds of being trapped,

Donald MacPherson B.E.M. photographed with two of the three loves of his life since his retirement, his garden and his dogs—the third love being his wife Betty.

and judging from my experience when I was torpedoed during the war and was submerged for a bit, I think drowning would be the nicest way to go. There has been an alarming rise in the fox population in the last few years and it's bad news for shepherds.

Then there is the dreaded 'Hoodie' the crow, with a beak on it like a nutcracker as I know to my cost. It has magnificent eyesight and can spot a ewe on her back from miles (or it seems like that) away. They go straight for a beast's eye, be it ewe, lamb, rabbit or whatever, and if they can get both they will. I've many a ewe that was 'couped' on her back that has lost an eye, who has come back into the flock after being set on her feet by myself or the shepherd, but she's never easy to be gathered again. In Mull they luckily don't have foxes, but all too many 'hoodies'. An old pal of mine who, like myself, is not so sprightly nowadays said, when I asked how he was getting on with the 'hoodie' problem: 'the hoodies and I have an agreement that they can have one twin as long as they leave me the singles'. I just hope they stick to their bargain, as they are the one breed of all our birds I hate. I've had problems with eagles, ravens, hen harriers and sparrow hawks, but they all have redeeming features mostly to do with their wonderful flying ability. Hating the hoodie crow as I do, I was annoyed after taking over the factorship of a well known Highland estate, when I was only in my thirties, to be likened to one. When I nervously asked the head keeper at our first meeting if he had any trouble with vermin, 'Only a puckle hoodies and a factor', was the reply. I know I've told this story before but I like it.

But back to my shepherds in April. Most hill farms had a wee bit of arable land, since tatties were an essential crop to keep the house folk fed in winter in the days when 'a tattie and neep and an ingin [onion]', as Harry Lauder used to sing, were the only veg. we saw in winter before the advent of the supermarket. Donald was taken on as a shepherd the moment he left school, but found that he was expected to do everything but work with the sheep. He was engaged on an Argyll farm that had some good arable land at sea level but also an extensive hill. There were fifty milking cows on it, and four folk, of which he was one, got up at 4 a.m. to milk them by hand, and as he says the hygiene was minimal. His wage was twenty shillings per week, but he was kept waiting six months before he got it in case he pushed off! April was when he hoped he would be at the lambing, but no, he was set to with another young lad to empty the cattle courts that were piled high with dung. There were no fore-loaders in these days, just manual, sweated (literally), labour. The dung, once deposited in the horse box carts, was driven out to the potato field which had already been drilled, and the dung was spread in the drills. Into the drills were planted the tatties, and what a wonderful taste a 'Kerr's Pink' or 'Golden Wonder' has if grown in that manner. Those who enjoy organic food would fall over backwards to buy them nowadays, but they would have to realise how labour-intensive that method is. These days you don't get laddies working for twenty shillings (£1.00) per week, and for all the hours of daylight. Then after the tattie planting the turnips had to be thinned, i.e. using a hoe one had to knock out enough turnips to leave one plant every nine inches, a painstaking and dreich job. Donald, like the author, thought it the most boring job on the farm, and the end of the drill always seemed a long, long way off!

Donald's pal, who had thought he was employed to learn shepherding and found he was just a dogsbody, decided to pack it in and said to the boss, 'When you advertise for my replacement, write "Navvy wanted, with slight knowledge of sheep"!'

May

When Pat told his father, back in the twenties, that he wanted to follow in his footsteps and be a shepherd, old Peter, after trying to dissuade him, as things were at rock bottom in farming then, gave him one bit of advice: 'Don't look at your boots, laddie, look around you.' To a townee this may sound stupid, as on a hill the ground is so uneven, but to a shepherd or anyone employed with stock this advice is gold dust. Only by looking around can one spot the dozens of disasters that can occur: a ewe couped (fallen onto her back and unable to rise), a lamb in a hill drain, a ewe having a difficult lambing etc.

Spring comes late in the high hills, and the shepherds herding them will still be busy lambing there well into the second and third week of May. There often used to be late snows, and snow would linger in the corries well into the summer. One of the farms on the Blackmount Estate which I managed, Glenoe in the shadow of Ben Cruachan, had many years ago a tenant called McIntyre (the Dukes of Argyll and the Marquises of Breadalbane, the chiefs of the mighty Campbell clan, always had smaller buffer clans round them to take the brunt of the first assault by any rival clan e.g. the MacDonalds). The McIntyres had a famous white cow, and the rent they had to pay for their farm was a white calf and a snowball taken from Ben Cruachan at the May term (28th). Ben Cruachan never let them down and always had snow in one of its north facing corries, but the white cow came to the end of her breeding days and couldn't deliver the rent. History relates that the McIntyres got the heave-ho!

But May for a hill shepherd is a magical month with the arrival of spring. As well as all the problems attendant to lambing there are added bonuses. The changing colours, grass turning green to feed the flock, the dippers, those sparkling little black and white birds darting up and down the Highland burns, and the black-headed gulls that come inland to nest. The eggs of the black-headed gulls are delicious, but they mob anyone who goes near their nesting area—Pat once saw an old dog fox getting a fearful doing from a flock of gulls. But it's the hills that all those of us who have worked in them just love, with their changing lights and their majesty as they seem to dominate us mere humans. No wonder the Psalmist wrote: 'I to the hills will lift mine eyes from whence doth come mine aid'.

As well as using his eyes, the shepherd hears so much that helps him in his job. That lamb calling for its mother, that fox bark that gives him an idea of the rough direction of its den, the croak of the raven that may lead him to some dead or dying ewe. But better by far is hearing the curlew, the peewit, the lark, that old cock grouse saying: 'Go-back, Go-back'. Yes, those of us who once herded the hills were lucky indeed, but I wonder how many now riding their four-wheeled bikes can see or hear as much as we did. I love the story of the American boy from the back-country who went to stay with his uncle in New York. They were walking up Fifth Avenue and the laddie said: 'Listen, uncle, to the cricket'. The uncle replied : 'Don't be silly, with all this traffic and noise how could you hear a cricket, and anyway where would one be'? The boy walked up to the nearest posh hotel which had two mulberry trees in tubs outside it, and picked the cricket out of one of them. The uncle then said: 'How on earth did you hear that?' to which the boy replied: 'Your ear hears what it's attuned to'. He then threw a dollar onto the pavement and at its clink everyone within fifty yards turned their heads! I fear that in our love for money we are becoming the same in this country.

But for all the beauty of May for the shepherd he can have problems. Those still lambing then can find that, as mentioned the April chapter, the 'couping' of ewes on their backs can be all too common. Sadly, many people who find a ewe on her back naturally think they are being kind by putting her straight back on her feet. However this can have serious consequences, because while she has been on her back the gases will have built up in her stomach. Before sheep are stood on their feet they should first be turned on their side for a while to let some of the gases escape. Some shepherds on farms that were noted for ewes getting couped used to carry a wooden spatula to let the gas out. Ewes that coup always seem to be ones on

Lambing goes on into May in many areas, but the month can have its own particular problems, for example the 'couping' of ewes as described in this chapter (Polly Pullar).

the thrive and so one seldom found this problem in the high hill hirsels. As a ewe thrives the grease rises in the fleece and this unbalances her, so if one could clip the ewe one did, as it stopped her couping again. With (sadly, in my opinion) 'the right to roam' about to become law, if any readers come upon a couped ewe and want to help, they should, as stated above, turn the ewe gently on her side and leave her for ten minutes before setting her on her feet.

I say sadly that 'the right to roam' is about to become law, because of my experience with the West Highland Way when, as Factor of the Blackmount Estate, I was representing the Fleming family. They owned the stretch of the West Highland Way from Bridge of Orchy to the Kingshouse hotel on the old General Wade road, a distance of eight miles. The Flemings couldn't have been nicer and gave complete approval to the scheme. What has happened? A very small percentage of walkers won't stick to the way but wander all over parts of the land that used to give the Estate ten or twelve stags and the same amount of hinds each year. Now, thanks to their wanderings in technicolored clothing, there isn't a deer to be found. Yet it never occurs to them who pays the rates and the wages and the upkeep of the cottages that keep people in the Highlands, so that townees can enjoy the West Highland Way and walks like it. As ever it's a small percentage that won't comply with the unwritten rules, and I'm sure my readers will not be among them. If on any of their walks they are able to help a coupit ewe to her feet it would be a help to any shepherd, as he will only see his hirsel at the best twice a day, and a coupit ewe can die in half an hour in an acute case.

Donald in his many years of shepherding came across few 'coupit' ewes, as the grazing in those high acid wet hills of Argyll is not as lush as that further inland and in the Lowland hills. The job he hated most was 'sloughing' the wool from the dead ewes, of which there were always all too many on those large, almost ranch-like, western sheep-runs. It seems so strange all these years later when it is hard to sell wool, that then the 'sloughed' wool was eagerly sought after by dealer-type folk and good prices were paid for it in cash. The money must have been good because Donald remembers recommending a fellow shepherd, who was on a part-time basis, to his boss as a permanent employee, and the boss said: 'No way, he didn't slough his dead ewes'. For some reason sloughed fleeces had a terrible smell which one found it very hard to get rid of. One Friday after they had been sloughing wool Donald and his pal were going to a dance and decided to help themselves to some sweet smelling stuff they had seen in their boss's bathroom to mask the aroma. The result wasn't quite as they had hoped as some of their partners were dubious about men who covered themselves in scent!

Bracken in those far off days was dealt with by squads cutting it twice a year. A right good job they did, as when one was gathering and getting near the fank one didn't want to wade through a forest of bracken. The first cut was in May and the next in August, and it did a world of good. Nowadays the job is done by spraying from a helicopter (or a helico-peter as Geordie Menzies called it) but this is very expensive. It's funny how bracken always starts off on goodish ground: some of the best Golden Wonder tatties I ever tasted were grown on ground which had bracken growing before. I think it was that great Nationalist, Wendy Wood, who said that the three curses of the Highlands were all 'B's'—'Bracken, Braxy and MacBraynes'. It will indeed be sad if bracken is allowed to take over the Highlands in certain areas. In the old days when cattle were the four-legged animals in the hills they trod down the young fronds and there was never much bracken. What there was was cut for bedding the byre in winter. Even in my time the acreage of it has expanded beyond belief.

The best eradicator of bracken I ever had were some Essex Saddleback sows who rooted out the rhizomes. It was the late Richard Roadnight, who instigated the out-wintered ark pig system that one sees today, who told me to try the pigs. Strange as it may seem, though I have judged cattle, ponies, sheep, overall championships (yes, and show queens) I have never been connected with the pig world. Yet despite this, since my retirement, I miss my 'piggies' more than any of the other stock I farmed. They loved to be scratched, always gave me a great welcome when I went into the byre to feed them first thing in the morning and, believe it or not, were by far the cleanest animals I have had to deal with. If one gave them a good straw bed in a corner they made their midden in another, whereas cattle and horses do their 'jobbies' any old place and the latters' dung has to be taken off the horse paddock each day for fear of red worm infection. I wish horses would follow the pigs' example and use one corner of the paddock!

But back to bracken, which was excellent bedding for the shepherd's house-cow so that he might well leave a good bed of the stuff not too far from his cottage. However, he would certainly make sure that the beds next to the fank were cut. Nowadays, how many modern shepherds have (a) a house cow or (b) can handle a scythe? The answer to (a) is only a very, very few in the remote areas; and (b) again the answer is very few, though many will have 'strimmers'. They won't bother about the upsurge of bracken in the area, which I predict will, as Wendy said all those years ago, turn out to be a curse. Happily braxy and MacBraynes are no longer curses: the first now has an injection to sort it out and the second has a super new boat on the Mull run that can take up to one thousand cars a day.

The old stone-walled sheep fanks, of which many excellent examples still survive, show how the old folk used their knowledge and their skills. The fanks had to be sited in the right place, a spot to which the sheep would run but also beside some knowe or hillock where ewes could be dried off before they were clipped. They were beautifully built, but the middle area where one handled the sheep was usually too large, and Donald put 'shedders' into all the fanks that he used. Shedders were small wooden lanes, each one of which only allowed a single line of sheep to progress through it. The direction of the sheep was always uphill, and at the top one had small gates which could either allow a sheep to run straight through, or, if the gate was pushed over smartly, to stop the sheep so that it came in behind the man operating the gate i.e. so that it was being shed from the main flock. One can organise a shedder in this way so that one can segregate five different categories of sheep at a time. Making new shedders or repairing the old ones and adding more gates was one of the jobs Donald liked to do in May.

Pat on the other hand had long finished lambing by this time. He remembers one year when his hoggs had come home from the wintering and the grass was slow to come. As a result he lost hoggs which had been bitten by adders. To me this sounds incredible, as I've only once seen an adder, back in the thirties on a hot August day. Pat reckons what happened on this occasion was that the keep was so scarce that the hoggs had to nosey about for food and the adders bit them on the tongue. Pat says he knew all the deaths were caused by adders as the hoggs all had pin holes in their tongues and their heads were swollen.

May was always a time for getting ready for the big gatherings in later months: the lamb marking and yeld sheep clippings in June and the gatherings for the 'milk clippings' in July. On gathering days bridges over burns, which can be all too full, are essential, so their maintenance was a must. The old bridges were 'turf tappit' i.e. had turf on their tops, but sadly the deer made a real mess of them and when corrugated iron came in the bridges didn't need half as much upkeep.

May too was the month when some shepherds wanted to move on, as in the old days the two movement dates were the May or the November terms i.e. the 28th day of those months. The reasons for moving were many. Perhaps a shepherd had had a disastrous lambing. I knew of one case where a shepherd had to dig holes to bury forty ewes because his boss was too mean to buy hay, which was the only feed we used then, in one of those terrible years in the fifties. Or it might have been that the boss and the shepherd, at the time when the shepherd was engaged, thought they would form a great partnership (which is absolutely essential in any type of business, especially farming) but found it just didn't work out. But no way, unlike modern football managers and players, would shepherds break their contracts once they were made. In the old days this was a word of mouth agreement that the shepherd would give a month's notice if he wanted to leave, and the boss would give him a month's notice if the shepherd hadn't come up to his expectations. There would be dozens applying for the vacant job fifty years ago, changed days indeed.

One of the longest journeys made to 'flit' from one job to another was by Pat's father, who came from the Island of Eigg to Glenartney, central Perthshire. The reason for his move was that he wanted to have a better education for his family—what a difference to all too many today who start off by wanting to know what the wages and perquisites are. Even in my day Scottish education was looked up to around the world, and until the last war the Scottish dominie (teacher) and his wife were in the top social group with the minister, the doctor and the lawyer. Sadly this has completely changed: the 'calling' to be a minister or a teacher has gone, and it is how much they can earn that matters to all too many people. I will never forget my father, a Church of Scotland minister, telling me that I would never do anything worthwhile in life because I had failed my veterinary exams. He would perhaps have been right, had it not been that the schooling that he got for me (which he could ill afford) has given me a career of fifty years in broadcasting among other things. Yes, education was all important in Scotland between the wars, and old Peter MacNab made a good move when he went to Glenartney. All his family did well, thanks to their education, and the fact that they met many more people than they could ever have done on Eigg.

The starting point of Peter's journey from Eigg was four miles distant from the pier, where their furniture had to be loaded on a wee boat called the *Foch* (we were still friendly with the French after the 1914–18 war, and the boat was named after one of their Generals). All their furniture was encased in hessian sacking, which had been saved up from all the many bags made of hessian then, and all beautifully sewn with the wool sack needles we used in those days. So off they set in the old box carts pulled by horses along gravel-tracked roads. The *Foch* sailed to Fort William, where the furniture was transported in hand barrows to the luggage van of the train which went to Callander. Then it was transferred to a train going back up the line to Balquhidder, Lochearnhead, St Fillans and Comrie. Sadly this line was 'Beechinged'—though how overseas visitors would have loved the run through Glenogle glen, which I was lucky enough to see from an observatory car at the rear of the train back in the late twenties. When Peter's furniture eventually arrived at Comrie it once more had to be moved by horse box-cart over gravel roads to Staghorn Cottage at the head of Glenartney. Here it was that they reared a first class family, and Peter did a fantastic job for the Earl of Ancaster, one which sadly was never properly appreciated, as labour was cheap then and dispensable. But just fancy doing that flitting to go to a job where you were to be paid thirty-six pounds per annum—any volunteers?

The May Term flittings were occasions for having the neighbours round, and hard up though everyone might be, a drop of the 'cratur' always seemed to be procured (especially in Speyside where I farmed 1951-59). I remember well a flitting of a crofter who was a first-class stocksman but idle as get out, who smoked his pipe all day. We were busy taking out his furniture to put on my and other farmers' tractor bogies while he stood, draped in an ancient 'mac' tied in the middle with binder twine, and looked on. All flittings needed a bonfire, as there was always so much rubbish to get rid of, and on this occasion the bonfire was threatening the wee but-an'-ben croft which had a thatched roof. I rushed out to the crofter and exclaimed: 'Where's the nearest water supply?' as there was no running water in the croft. As long as I live I will never forget his reply: 'Have you seen my tobacco, Captain Ben?'

Yes, flittings could be dramatic occasions. The word 'occasion' then meant not only a flitting but could describe a wedding, a funeral (quite the most drunken 'occasions' I encountered in the Highlands were when one toasted the deceased, no matter how much you couldn't thole the person when alive) or a christening—oh! just any excuse for a 'spree'. Times were hard fifty years ago, and if a bottle could be found, whether it had been presented for a shepherd's crook made, as a back hander for a beast bought worth the money, or for some work done for a neighbour—or better still if it was some of that lovely 'mother's milk', the clear stuff from the distillery where one had been getting the 'draff' to feed one's cows—it didn't matter how a drop of the 'cratur' was procured, it was kept for an 'occasion'. The poor wives were expected to do their stuff, no equality of sexes then. They were expected to produce a good meal for the neighbours who came to help, and of course this had to be better than the one laid on by Mrs 'X' when she had been flitted from the neighbouring farm. One shepherd's wife was so fed up with the whole scene that at the end of the meal she took the ends of the table cloth together, gathering up all the cups, butter, jam etc., put a rope around it, threw it on top of the cart that contained the flitting and said: 'I'm off'. History doesn't relate if she was seen again.

There were no Pickfords or their like in those days, and had there been no one could have afforded them, but some carters were especially good at the job. They would come in the late afternoon, 'lowse' their horse and get a bit 'stob' or pole around which they would hitch the 'rigwoodie', i.e. the chain that goes from one shaft to the other and fits into the horse's saddle. They then would load the two box carts (there were usually two) in the evening ready to leave at 4 a.m. the next morning. I have built loads of sheaves of corn onto box carts that had an extra extension put on for the purpose, and I know how important it was to build the load so that there wasn't too much weight on the horse's back, or too much on the back of the cart so that it would almost lift the horse off the ground (thanks to the belly band underneath him). So I know from experience that these men must have been past masters at their job, firstly in building their loads and secondly in yoking the horses the next morning at 4 a.m. There can't be many, if any, still alive today, but if they were I'll bet some of the big re-moval firms would snap them up. They certainly knew how to pack in furniture, furniture which in many cases had already been moved all too many times.

But given a good lambing and a good month weather-wise, a shepherd could look forward to June when his lambs would be counted. There was no use a shepherd thinking he had had a good lambing until the June mark-ings and I've seen many sad faces on shepherds who thought they had done well. But 'the proof of the pudding is in the eating' and it's the lambs that come in to be marked that are the ones that count.

June

June was one of the hardest months for a hill shepherd, as there were constant gatherings to mark the lambs and to clip the hoggs and yeld ewes. In the old days before contractors did the clipping every farm 'neighboured' with the farms next to them and it was essential that the neighbours were properly fed and watered, quite apart from the home staff. The farmers' wives were an integral part of the operations. Some were super and some were absolutely bloody awful. I remember well on one estate I managed, the wife of one the shepherds (a good hand) was known as the 'Black Minorca' (after a black breed of hen) because she had never been known to clean a pot in her life! Then there was the wife of another who was given a gigot of lamb to feed the hungry mob, didn't know what to do with it and boiled it instead of roasting it. She then proudly told an elderly shepherd's wife, who was a super cook: 'There didn't seem to be any gravy when I boiled it, so I put in some axle grease'. I'm surprised the shepherd who told me the story is still alive, but they bred the McCallums hardy in those days!

But the main reasons for the June gatherings were to count and mark the lambs, and to clip the ewe hoggs and the yeld ewes as by then their fleeces would have enough 'rise' for one to shear them. At this time of year the new wool starts to rise and has gained enough growth to allow one to shear through it with hand shears, which is all we had fifty years ago. The ewes with lambs at foot are not fit to clip for another month, as they are giving everything they can to their lambs, not to their wool.

Every Scottish Highland sheep farm has a 'lug-mark', i.e. a clipping taken out of the ear of the lamb on the lamb-marking day which denotes on which farm it was born. There is a wonderful old book which records every lug mark in Scotland, but sadly I haven't got a copy. Nor have I a retentive memory for 'lug-marks' as had old Peter, the head yardsman in the now defunct MacDonald, Fraser mart in Glasgow. I was selling lambs there in the sixties from the Ardkinglas Estate, and when the next pen to ours was being filled Peter said to the consignor: 'There are two lambs there that don't belong to you, they come from XYZ farm, I can see by their lug mark'. Absolutely brilliant. He was just a chap who was only reckoned to be good enough to be a yardsman, but he would have done well in MI5. And that's what 'lug-marks' were all about, because during the years, especially in war-time, when sheep and wool are wanted, you will get the unscrupulous farmer or dealer who wants to make the fast buck.

The Highland Show, now the Royal Highland Show, has always been the tops for Scots who love either showing, judging, doing a T.V. pro-gramme, or just socialising with fellow farmers to hear their moans (of those there are always plenty). I've attended almost all since the first one post-war in Inverness, when I drove an old ex-army lorry with Beef Shorthorns from Millhills, Crieff, and it took damned nearly a day. Since then when I was managing Highland estates I found that all too often the marking gatherings clashed with the Highland Show. As one always 'neighboured' in those days, to get through a whole district took at least a fortnight out of the end of the month of June, and some farm was bound to have its gathering in Highland Show week. When I went to Gaskbeg, Lagganbridge, at the head of the Spey, in 1951, there were six farms which 'neighboured', and as last joined I was 'Tail-end Charlie'. As a result my gathering nearly always landed in Highland Show week, but I always managed to postpone things. And when I left eight years later I was still at the end of the line.

The farm which had elected to be first often hit one of the cold spells that we can get in the Highlands at that time of year, but luckily then we only had hand shears to clip the hoggs and yeld ewes, and with them there is still a bit of wool left on the sheep, unlike with electric shears where one is shearing very close to the skin. Even as it was they occasionally had a dead hogg or two, after all it was land over one thousand feet above sea level.

There were two things which always worried me about the June gatherings. The first was the difficulty of getting all the lambs in the fank: there were always some that broke back, as it was the first time they had been gathered and they had no fear of the collies. The second was the time it took to 'mother up' a neighbour's ewe with its lamb. To solve the first problem I got a huge long roll of hessian sheeting about a yard high and made the shepherds hold it in front of them making a sort of semi-circular wall, but even with that some lambs broke away. The whole procedure could be a long time-consuming business. The reason one had to do it was that the high Highland sheep farms have no march fences, and although 99% of the ewes are 'hefted' to their hirsel, some stray onto the neighbour's ground and come into their neighbour's marking gatherings with their lambs at foot. Some shepherds were extremely clever at shedding the neighbour's ewes and lambs off before they ever got into the main gathering, and others, usually with extra good dogs, managed to put a mark on the neighbour's lambs before they got to the fank. Always, however, there were some neighbours' ewes (known by their keel and lug marks) that had to be 'mothered up', and this could take ages. The lambs were completely disorientated as they had never been gathered before; but the job had to be done otherwise one would be putting one's lug mark on a neighbour's lambs. A few unscrupulous farmers did so, but it was looked on as sheep stealing (punishable by death two hundred years ago) by the majority.

After those long but wonderful gatherings how one longed for one's breakfast. Talking of wonderful I remember a magical morning when I was on the top of Ben Ime, part of Ardkinglas Estate in Argyll, and I felt I was on the roof of Scotland as I could see Ben Nevis to the north, Goatfell in Arran to the south and many, many 'Munroes' in between. But back to the breakfast, and it depended on which shepherd's wife (if it was a big estate) or farmer's wife (if it was farmers who were neighbouring) it was, as to how good it would be. I well remember getting stuck into some jelly to put on my 'piece' one day, and then noticing that not one of the eight other gatherers were having any jelly at all. When I got outside I said to the head shepherd: 'What was wrong with the jelly?' To which he replied: 'We were here and you weren't, Captain, when she was making it, and she was straining it through her knickers'. Well, you could have fooled me.

When the sheep were in the fank they were shed off into their respective lots, the lambs to be marked, the hoggs and the ewes (making a helluva noise because they were missing their lambs) to be shorn. All the lambs had to be lug-marked and have their tails docked. The males had to be castrated as well on the majority of farms, because out of all the sheep farms in Scotland few specialise in tup breeding. So the lambs were herded into an area where they were caught by the shepherd, usually the head man or the farmer's shepherd. He held two legs of the lamb with one hand and two with the other hand, then put the lamb on a board that had been placed on top of the shedder so that the lamb's tail and testicles (if any) were hanging over the board. The person, often me, who was doing the lug marking, tail shortening and castrating was on the other side of the fence. I can imagine townees thinking how cruel all this was, but in all the years I've lug-marked, docked and castrated lambs, I've only had one lamb that didn't run away bellowing for its Mum. This is why I tell the 'do-gooders' that they are so wrong to think that animals feel pain as we do. Just try some of the things we do to lambs on humans and the latter would faint if not die.

The reason we lug mark is to identify the lamb's origin. The reason we dock their tails is that if they are left long the tails get dung on them. This attracts the blue fly which produce maggots: these burrow into the sheep and eventually kill them in a lingering death. The reason we castrate the lambs is that one can't have hundreds of rams practising incest and producing worse and worse in-bred sheep—nor does one want to produce 'ram mutton', which is extremely strong in taste and smell.

Times have changed as far as castration is concerned. Nowadays rubber rings are used which stop the blood flow and cut off the nervous system to the testicles. I think it a retrograde step, as I've seen dozens of lambs writhing in pain after they've had a rubber ring put on their scrotum, whereas I can remember in the old days when we used the knife the lambs used to jump up and run off. In my young days the testicles were drawn by your teeth, and as most of the old shepherds had a rotten tooth or two which might infect the lamb, and others had 'falsies', I did more than my share of castrating. The testicles were known as 'sweetbreads' to us, and were absolutely delicious (when cooked), but with the modern rubber ring the lamb goes through more pain and we don't get our sweetbreads! In the north where sweetbreads were not eaten the dogs used to sit around in circles waiting for the only protein, apart from the ewe's afterbirth, they got all year.

To a person who hasn't worked on the land along with nature this all must sound very crude, but it's the sad thing about all too many who come to the country from a town background that they don't realise how cruel nature can be. One only has to see a weasel mesmerising a rabbit before it kills it, or one hoodie crow acting as a decoy to take off a mother peewit while its mate goes off with the chick etc., etc., to realise sometimes one must be cruel to be kind.

But back to the June gatherings, and let's take a look at the lug marking. Some older shepherds were marvellous at the job, using a sharp knife and getting the 'lug' between it and their horny thumb. There were marks called 'back half' (sounds like part of some phoney rugby team), 'fore half', 'fork' which is self explanatory, and 'crop', whereby an unscrupulous farmer could cut off half the lug, and so it was known as the sheep stealers' lug mark. I don't think the late Earl of Ancaster would have liked to have known that his famous Corrychrone hirsel had a crop as its lug mark. Then there was the 'nip', not so easy to make with a knife, but one got miniature forceps to do the job. Pat, Donald and I think we made a better job of downing other sorts of 'nips', preferably with chasers, after the long day's work was done— and the days *were* long as we had started at four or five a.m.

As I have said, the 'mothering-up' process could be a lengthy one, as you can imagine how lost the lambs would be. It was their first taste of being gathered, they had been suddenly weaned, albeit temporarily, from their mums, been lug marked, had their tails docked and, if male, castrated, and only then let go to find the 'Milk Bar'. But nature is wonderful, and I'm a lucky laddie to have worked alongside it (and, I might say, not against it like all too many farmers) for all my life. Just imagine anything up to four hundred lambs exploding out of a fank to find their mothers, and yet in the morning one would find at worst four or five that hadn't managed to do so. To humans all the lamb bleats sound the same but not to the ewe.

And talking of nature, I often wonder if we humans have tried to be too clever. Nowadays, with the aim of getting a bigger calf in certain breeds, they have to have horrible large corkscrew-type machines for extracting the huge calves from their mothers, whereas neither Pat, Donald nor I have ever seen a red deer hind that needed help at their June calving. Pat said his Dad once had to calve a hind in a peat bog, but it was after a terrible winter and the hind was so lean Peter was certain she wouldn't survive. He never saw her or the calf when next he was round that way, so they must have at least stumbled out of the peat bog. I used to love coming across a new-born fawn with its white spots. The hinds are so clever in the way they hide their fawns in tall bracken or some other good hiding place and go off and graze to make the milk for the fawn. The wee animals were so shy and, although probably terrified, looked up at one with those lovely soft eyes they have.

Are 'fawn-like' eyes not famous—and yet I wonder how many have seen them in real life!

Talking of eyes, when I told Pat I was writing about old Peter in MacDonald and Frasers Mart, Glasgow, Pat recalled: 'I sold him a dog once with an amber eye. Never have a dog with an amber eye. This one could be marvellous, work all day, plenty of force, which Peter wanted in the mart, and then the next day would spend all the time in the world with one old ewe and a lamb down by a burn and I would have to go and fetch him. Never trust one with an amber eye!'

Going back to the lambs being mothered-up and how lost they looked, there is no doubt that the less one had to gather ewes and lambs at foot the better the lambs were at sale time in September. Ewes also, if left alone and not fed, can often lamb more easily on their own. 'Why then did you do all that gathering and spend so much time at the lambing?' the townee may rightly ask. The answer, quite simply, is that even fifty years ago we wanted to reach the standard of living that we thought we deserved. Compared to today's standards this was peanuts, but the extra lambs that could be saved made all the difference to the farm's income. Pre-war there were one hundred Edinample ewes on the back of Ben Vorlich that were never herded, and they were gathered late on with a more than useful lamb crop. However there were fewer foxes and hoodies then, as the area was well keepered and they were lightly stocked. Today, with the ridiculous headage subsidy payment, all too many hirsels are overstocked. Sadly already the 'neighbouring' has gone, except in a very few remote areas. What fun it all was, all the vying with each other as to who had the best lambs, hoggs and ewes and the competition about how one would fare at the local mart where one sold one's stock. Then on a large estate there was the rivalry between hirsels as to who had the highest lambing percentage. These were days I'll never forget and these are the conditions that have made Scotland and its people, who after all started as a nation with a background from the land and the stocks that grazed it. Now we in-winter and pamper our stock, and in many cases import breeds that need cosseting. The result may have given more profit to the owners but has done nothing for the type of Scot that used to herd our Scottish hills, more's the pity.

Then, of course, after one had lug-marked, tailed and castrated, the hoggs and yeld ewes had to be clipped. As July is the month for the main 'milk' clipping I don't want to go into too much detail in this chapter, but how things have changed. I remember only too well back in the fifties, when I was managing the Cluny Estate at the head of the Spey, and I couldn't get a

Pat and Donald getting ready to shear a hogg.

*Donald is seated on the last remaining clipping stool at Ardkinglas and is
shearing with a pair of hand shears under the watchful eye of Pat. The shed
they are in was built as a multi-purpose sheep shed. The gate behind Pat
opens into a 'bucht' from which the modern shearer will 'crog' his own
sheep. The slats in the wall, or Yorkshire boarding as it is called, allow for
the passage of air but keep the worst of the elements out, so that ewe hoggs
can be inwintered in the shed.*

wife to feed the neighbouring clippers. Instead I employed a certain Alexander MacLarty (known as 'the Fox' locally) and his team to come and do the clipping on contract, and he had a team of first-class hand clippers. Well, you would have thought the end of the world had come, as I got stick from all my neighbours. I hated doing it, but it was the start of what is now the norm on all sheep farms, Lowland and Highland. Wives now said, when asked to help out with the neighbouring: 'Sorry, I've got a job'.

Back in those days we all clipped by hand with shears, 'blades' as they were called by the Aussies and New Zealanders, who were ahead of us in using electric shears and now do a lot of the contract shearing in Scotland. One sees the occasional photo from the days of the original turf shearing stools, with those lovely old shepherds and their beards, who look to me as if they should have been on the stool and not the sheep!

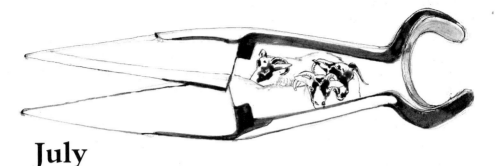

July

July is and always has been the clipping month, especially for hill shepherds. The other two 'musketeers' have, however, rightly taken me to task for not mentioning in my June chapter the bother they used to have with maggots at the marking gathering and thereafter, which necessitated clipping the milk ewes' tails. Until 1952, with the introduction of Dieldrin dip, maggots were the biggest enemy a shepherd had to face. That menace I'll deal with in more detail in a later chapter, but I know only too well what a pest it must have been to turn all the ewes at the marking gathering to clip the dung off their tails.

But back to the 'milk clippings' in July, a time of hard work, neighbour-liness (as always), the swapping of gossip and news (no T.V. then) and fun. I remember so well as a boy at St Fillans, in the days when my one ambition was to play rugger for Scotland, I was more than willing to spend days 'crogging' i.e. taking the ewes from the fank to those who were to shear them. Old Jock Ferguson the farm manager used to open the fank gate to allow each ewe to leap in the air, as they always do, and then to be caught by yours truly, which was wonderful practice for tackling an opponent on the rugby field.

As at the marking gathering the ewes and lambs had first to be gathered off the hill. Now, from what I see moving round the country, all too many ewes and lambs are kept 'inbye', below the hill proper, until after the milk clipping, adding to their worm burden and dirtying land that we used to use either to make hay from or, if not good enough for that, we would keep it clean and use it to draw the best of the lambs for market.

Gathering for the milk clipping could be badly hampered on the lower ground of some hirsels by the beds of bracken. Donald remembers a shepherd, who had served in the Far East in the last war, saying to him when he finished gathering one hirsel: 'I'd rather go through the jungle in Burma than that bloody bracken!' It's extraordinary the hold bracken has taken in the Highlands since the old bracken-cutting grant was taken off. Strange how two of the best grants we had for hill farming have vanished, that one and the lime and slag subsidy, which resuscitated thousands of acres of acid soil. Could it be that the influential voices backing the farming cause in the last fifty years have come from those with a big stake in the good arable acres of this fertile island of ours?

Another thing that made the milk clipping gathering a bit dodgy was that the lambs were older and bolder and not so dependent on Mum. As before, once in the fank, the flock had to be 'shed' off so that the ewes, lambs, hoggs and stragglers were all separate from one another, and then one had to wait until the ewes were dry. With the vast amount of sheds that have been erected in the country, and I've been responsible for building some of them, many, many hours of wasted time have been saved. Often in the old days one got the sheep gathered and dried and a nasty shower, all too common in July, would soak them again.

On the subject of sheds, all too many are ghastly blots on the landscape. I'm proud to say that, thanks to the late John Noble (brother of Michael, Secretary of State for Scotland, and his partner in running the Ardkinglas Estate), the clipping shed I had built at Butterbridge, at the head of the Rest and Be Thankful, not only is standing to this day, but because I was made to use imported wooden tile shingles instead of cheaper corrugated iron or asbestos, it blends into the surrounding scenery. Sadly, because the persons who inherited the property cleared the sheep (and the shepherds), the clipping shed is not being used for the purpose for which it was built, more's the pity.

I always remember when I advertised for a shepherd for Butterbridge. During the time I was managing the Ardkinglas Estate in 1959-64, few married shepherds wanted to be in isolated places, as they had seen on T.V. another way of life that the wives thought they would prefer. As a result when I advertised for a shepherd I got a middling lot of applicants. Butterbridge is smack on the main road from Glasgow to Campbeltown, but miles from the nearest village of Cairndow. How things have changed: now people who have tasted the hassle and crowding in our cities are queuing up to come to the country. I have met all sorts of people who in my young days would have been professionals, i.e. doctors, lawyers, church ministers (oh yes, in the twenties that was a highly thought of profession) et al, but who now want mud on their hands and feet instead and are small farmers, keepers, shepherds etc.

Sheep-shearing at Butterbridge, Glenkinglas, about the year 1900.

A STICK, HILL BOOTS AND A GOOD COLLIE DOG

Well, the best of a middling bunch of applicants for the shepherd's job was a person who had been brought up in the town but didn't like it. He had been well educated but had left his home and gone shepherding on one of our Scottish islands. His references said he had good dogs (an essential) and that he was married. Both turned out to be untrue, and not for the first time I learned to mistrust references. In my later days of management I relied only on telephone calls, as all too often the written references gave only the good points (if any) of the candidate and didn't mention the man's failings. The best telephone reference I ever had was from George Grant, Blacksboat, Ballindalloch, when I phoned and asked about one Robbie McHardy. George said: 'If I had a job for him you wouldn't get him'. On that occasion I got the best friend it's been my fortune to make, who worked for me for twenty five years and whom I still sorely miss. He was like so many shepherds of the old school, full of commonsense, a great naturalist, dead honest, a perfectionist when he did a job, it had to be right, and loyal till the day he died. I may be cynical but I think they've lost the mould from which these men were made, but I'm lucky in having two of them helping me with this book.

The shepherd I feed for the Butterbridge job had few of the old-type shepherds' characteristics. His so-called wife turned out to be a 'bidey in' (Scots for a partner), which forty years ago was frowned on in the Highlands although now anything goes! She was however a 'cordon bleu' cook, which Michael Noble and I, who both loved our food, thought would be a nice change from the 'Black Minorca's' cooking. I wasn't present at the first meal she produced, but I got a strong complaint from those who were there that she had tried to poison them all with rhododendron leaves. When I investigated, these turned out to be bay leaves! Forty years (plus) on I suppose workers now would want Chinese, Indian, Thai cooking, you name it—good old mince and tatties are no longer up-market enough.

Well, as usual I have strayed from my main subject, in this case the milk clippings, but all my off-beat stories have something to do with my main theme, in this case what a difference sheds made to those big clipping days. Before their advent one spent ages moving ewes backwards and forwards over knowes to let the air get under them to dry the fleece. Donald tells a lovely story of the days when he was starting as a herd laddie. They'd all been up at 4 a.m., and gathered the hirsel on the sort of day one can get in Argyll in July, dry in the morning but possible showers later on. They got their breakfast and the farmer sent the older men to herd the ewes onto the knowes to dry them. To the gang that was left he said: 'Those with coats go to thin the neeps.' The young lads who weren't earning enough to afford coats were winking to each other and having a quiet giggle thinking they'd been let off the hook, when, after a short interval, their boss went on, 'And those without coats can follow them.' I've recounted already how Donald and I thought this the worst job in farming.

Pat, on the other hand, was never on a sheep farm which had turnips to thin, but reckons, just as Donald did, that it was degrading for a shepherd to go thinning neeps. He had, after all, clipped hundreds if not thousands of sheep, and had to pack the wool for six New Zealand shearers. About this he said: 'I've never lost more sweat in my life'. From my experience of being in charge of big clipping days in Scotland and, as a Nuffield Scholar, representing Scotland in the International Wool Secretariat at the Godfrey Bowen shearing school in New Zealand, I realise Pat's employers were asking him to do the impossible.

But from the modern Godfrey Bowen shearing technique, back to the milk clippings of those far off days. At that time many fanks had permanent shearing stools, which both Donald and Pat remember were rather like low stone dykes. They were 'turf tappit'—built of stones with a layer of turf on top that had grown together. Pat clipped on one and said it needed a nice fleece for the shearer to sit on otherwise it could be cold and uncomfortable. Then came the shearing stools like the one which you see illustrated in the previous chapter. After that the young chaps started clipping on the ground, and from there we have moved on from hand shears to using electric combs, rather similar to those used by modern barbers!

It was amusing hearing the two 'oldies' discussing how the hand shears had degenerated over the years. The old ones were made of black steel, but one of my pals thought the more modern ones resembled 'a load of old manure' (only using another word for it). Another thing we all agreed on about the old hand shearing was how some first-class clippers just couldn't sharpen their shears. I sadly was good at neither, although I've been clipping sheep for more than fifty years. As for sharpening anything, I always seem to take the edge off rather than put it on a blade, but I've been blessed with good mates who have always come to the rescue.

Anyway, in the days of the stool clipping I found I could do much more good by going round inspecting any ewes with bad feet that needed paring, or those with an abnormality. Perhaps a beast had become 'soo-moothed' (i.e. with an undershot under jaw like a sow) or 'shaun gabbit', with an overshot under jaw. In this case the beast would have a special keel put on it so that we would know that it had to be cast before the next breeding season. Probably, dear reader, you may think that any deformities should have been spotted earlier, but believe me it wasn't easy if one was herding hundreds of sheep in 'miles and miles of damn all', when the only time one was close to one's hirsel was at the gatherings and then there was always an almighty rush. Going round as I did to inspect the ewes and encourage the clippers, I couldn't help but see the difference between the 'steady as you go' types and the ones that knocked off the first five or six fleeces and then spent much of the rest of the day sharpening their shears, gossiping to their neighbours or waiting for the bottle to come round, if one was clipping on a farm or estate that could afford such a luxury.

Inevitably one made the odd cut, but nothing like those I saw made in Australia where the shearers were operating on numbers shorn. Over there, however, they assured me they didn't have the fly problem we have. Here in the old days we used to dab Archangel Tar, which was in a big tin, onto cuts, and this was done either by a boy or someone who wasn't fit to clip, often a gamekeeper or farm or estate worker. He would use a stick with a wad of hessian tied on the end of it, for all the world like the modern microphones used in outside T.V. broadcasts. So when a clipper was finished, if he had 'nicked' a sheep he would shout 'Tar'. The fleece would then be taken away to be rolled and packed in those huge wool sacks. This was only done if the fleeces were dry, and we can all remember having to hang fleeces over fences to dry them off. I can't see many going to that bother today, for all that wool is worth.

Compared with man-made fibres wool is such a natural thing, I wish more people would use it in some form or other. But I doubt it, as recently I saw two hundred-plus people queuing for the Isle of Mull ferry on their return from a day visit to Iona, and every one seemed to be casually dressed in the sort of clothing made of man-made fibre that seems to be *de rigueur* today. A change from the time I first went to Mull to oversee three estates in the early fifties, and every one of us in the open ferry that took us from the *Lochinvar* to Criagnure wore tweed, including George MacLeod who resurrected the Abbey in Iona. Come to think of it, one of the ladies not only wore tweeds but had hairy stockings and smoked a pipe! The local wool in the old days was keenly sought after, in fact the Italians thought so much of the Blackface wool that a usual wedding present was a mattress made of it.

To satisfy the demand for wool, and also mutton, many hill farms kept wedders until they were three years old, which gave the owner three fleeces, always heavy. Pat talks of the days when the third draw of wedder lambs was retained and wintered on the arable ground around Drummond Castle in

Strathearn. They always lived well, and ninety-eight would come back out of the hundred sent down. As three-year-olds the Auchinner of Glenartney wedders always made the top price at the Stirling wedder sale. But Donald, not to be beaten, tells us how the Ardkinglas three-year-olds topped the Oban Sale in 1952. But tastes change, and no longer is wool or mutton as popular. Now it is a hard job to find just one wedder to send to the Queen Mum, who appreciates good-tasting mutton, whereas forty-five years ago one could have found thousands.

Once shorn, the wool is rolled and must be free of straw etc. Rolling wool is a specialised job, and rightly the Wool Board want it to be done properly. To this end they started demonstrations at different shows to illustrate how it should be done, and my brother Philip, who was the Scottish Wool Board officer at the time, and I ran a series of these demos at various shows including the Royal Highland. Even up to quite recently some small farmers and crofters used to tie up the fleeces with binder twine, with disastrous results! Donald was recalling how on one occasion he and his fellow young shepherds, way back, thought they were being clever in packing between fifty and sixty fleeces in a wool sack until they were told to carry them down to the road. No vehicle, not even a horse and cart, could get up to the old fank that had been sited, correctly as were all old fanks, at a place to which the sheep could easily be gathered. As Donald said, 'we thought we were carrying lead'. About thirty-four fleeces would be the norm for those old jute bags that ended up being used for more than just packing with wool, as all too many were pinched by farmers because they were beautifully made.

Another thing that has changed is that all the wool is now collected, sometimes late in the season, by haulage contractors. When I was in Gaskbeg between1951 and 1958 I used to go to Edinburgh to a firm called Leggats in the Dean Bridge, having driven my ancient Austin wartime lorry a great number of miles. There I would bargain gently about the price, partake of the essential dram or two, make them stand me lunch, get them to feed me with some material for my weekly 'Farm Forum' broadcast and then I'd drive back all those twisty miles of the old A9. How civilised all that way of doing business was, compared with today's philosophy of 'the de'il tak' the hinmost' in the modern farming scene.

Then came the advent of the modern way of shearing which is carried out by contractors. To begin with these were New Zealanders and Australians, but now it is done by our own lads. When the shearing machines first were introduced to this country from the Antipodes in the late fifties, in

Clipping course held at Clachan Farm (now the Oyster Bar), Cairndow, Argyll, for young shepherds in 1961 to show them how to use the new electric combs. Of the 21 shepherds on the course only three remained actively engaged with sheep in 1998. As well as the young shepherds the author appears at the far right of the back row, Donald third from the left on the back row and Lady Glenkinglas who organised the grub second from the left on the second row. The rest are either college officials or estate shepherds who gathered the sheep for the course.

conjunction with the West of Scotland Agricultural College I ran a course for young shepherds on how to shear with them. Twenty-one attended, of whom sadly only three are still connected with hill farming today. By the time I had organised the course the machines were electrically-operated, but the early versions were driven by an engine. Pat remembers an occasion when Bill Black, the well known band leader but formerly a shepherd, and others were shearing at Corrychrone, and the engine powering the shears was so hot and noisy the shepherds all wanted to go back to the old 'blades'. During the trials to perfect the electrically-operated models a Mr Yellowlees used to try out his prototypes on the Ardkinglas sheep—in the course of his experiments he nearly blew himself up and did himself no good. Then in came the overseas contractors who demanded that fanks be redesigned, so that each shearer had his own pen from which he could 'crog' his own sheep. The pen had to have a door with a spring on it through which the shearer could back in and out to collect his animal. They were paid by the number they sheared, an average of 250 to 300 a day compared with what we used to do with hand shears, around 120 a day at most.

We in Scotland have many shearers of world class standard, of which we have every reason to be proud, but they miss what we 'oldies' loved, which was the crack, the camaraderie and the lack of the sense of urgency that they feel today as they bash on from one farm to another. As they always say in the Highlands, the Gaelic word for tomorrow hasn't the same sense of urgency as the Spanish word 'mañana'! But time marches on. One can't turn the clock back, but the old clipping days were hard work and a lot of fun.

The biggest day's clipping that I knew of in my time was on the Ancaster Estate above Callander, which I wrote about in my book *Bred in the Highlands*. There were forty six men shearing, all with hand shears, and two gamekeepers, good friends of mine, were also employed. Alastair MacIntyre was 'crogging', and although he was more than used to hard work, at the end of the day his hands were raw flesh. The other, Archie MacNaughton, packed sixty four bags of wool, which I'm sure must be a national record. Pat was continuously gathering hirsel after hirsel, and had but two hours of sleep in between times. They bred them tough in those days.

August

When I wrote in one of my earlier chapters that Bracken, Braxy and MacBraynes were the three worst things to beset Argyll I was taken to task by Donald who said when he was a lad he was taught that the three were 'the Campbells, rabbits and midges'. Well, from my experience over in that county I would agree with the last of the three, as especially where there are rhododendrons the Argyll midges are the most vicious I know. It always amuses me now when people with money, and there seem to be plenty about as I write in 1998, are wanting out of London, the land agents show them those lovely photos of 'desirable properties' in the West Highlands. They are obviously taken in late May or early June when the rhodies and house are looking superb, but there is no mention of what it is like in August, when for a shepherd or anyone working outside the midges can be horrific. My experience of the area is that I once had to do a report on the Argyll Estates farming enterprises, back in the fifties, for which I was well paid, but sadly one of their employees who was as straight as Harry Lauder's stick scuppered it. As things have turned out, if my report had been adhered to the Argyll Estates would have greatly benefited.

Rabbits have come and gone depending on how bad the myxomatosis outbreak was in the area. I certainly got a lot more clean grazing at Gaskbeg in upper Speyside after I introduced a myxy rabbit from Strathearn in the fifties, as it's not a case of what the wee devils eat, it's what they soil. As for Campbells, not being a MacDonald, I don't have that inbuilt anti-Campbell feeling.

For me in my young days, August, with its thundery, 'mochy' weather, was the month for maggots. I remember very clearly helping a local shepherd at St Fillans, Perthshire, on a farm that had all too much bracken. I was still a schoolboy and on holiday, so it must have been the late twenties or early thirties. The number of ewes struck was horrific, and all we had to dress them with was stuff called 'Tom the Vet', but as the coarse old shepherd said, 'you might as well pee on them, Ben'. 'Tom the Vet' had a nice antiseptic sort of smell, but apart from soothing the broken skin did nothing to kill the maggots.

Pat and Donald when comparing notes on their younger days and the treatment of sheep for maggots reckoned they would be treating over a hundred a day. You can imagine how disheartening that must have been for young shepherds, because once the maggots had burrowed into the skin that animal was flawed for life and would be worth so much less at its sale time. Be it a lamb or a ewe every animal has to be sold off a hill farm sooner or later. I had used 'Tom the Vet', but the other two had 'Balsam and Sulphur' which was just as useless. Salvation came in 1952 when Dieldrin dip came in. This killed the bluebottle that laid the eggs that bred the wee maggots with the black rings round their middles, which burrowed into the skin of a sheep within a few hours of being hatched. None of the three of us, as you can imagine. are entomologists, but we reckon that the maggots we had then were entirely different from the ordinary fat white ones seen now.

When a sheep was struck it always made for water. Good old nature, she's always right, because drowning the maggots was in the old days the only way to get rid of them—but as I was to find to my cost could also get rid of the sheep. The occasion was when I was farming in upper Speyside and was neighbouring with a farmer who grazed wethers on Ben Alder. I had at the time a rather good dog, although I'm a rotten dog handler. This dog was a cast-off from the legendary Jim Wilson, who is the only man that has won three International Shields, i.e. nine wins, three for each shield). The reason he was a cast-off was he had too much force to be a trial dog. Because of my dog I was to take in the bottom part of the Ben which runs beside Loch Ericht, as on that bit there was a wether which was five or six years old, hadn't been clipped, and was notorious for escaping the gatherings by taking on the gathering dogs. When I came on the infamous animal he looked not only huge because of his various fleeces but was obviously maggoted. I already had some sheep gathered in front of me, and with 'Glen' between him and the Loch I thought I had him: but no way, he made straight for the Loch with 'Glen' hanging onto the wool around his neck. I

The author at Gaskbeg in 1951, with a few of the ewes that he took over. At this time he had not yet had a chance to improve the stock.

nearly lost the best dog I ever had along with my neighbour's ancient wether, as it tried to swim but instead sank without trace.

I know I'm taking up a lot of this chapter with talk about maggots, but modern shepherds don't realise how lucky they are not to have them to the same extent we had. The smell of them was ghastly and remained with one for all too long. Donald remembers coming home to find them in his boots. All the 'three musketeers' fancied their chance with the ladies in those far off days, but the smell of maggots wasn't, shall we say, comparable to Chanel No. 5!

Dieldrin worked wonders, and it was a disaster for the sheep industry when it was banned. According to Pat one old wifie in an outer isle found an eagle's egg sterile because it contained D.D.T., and when the law to ban the stuff came in front of the House of Commons there were all too few present. Whether this is true or false I know not, but all I can say is that we now have an organo-phosphorous dip that has maimed some humans for life, and for all I know may have hastened their death. Are we to put the lives of eagles and other raptors who preyed on carcasses which contained D.D.T. above the lives of humans?

In the old days a shepherd was always going round his hirsel, and as sure as God made little apples he'd come on some animal or other with a problem, whereas nowadays the shepherds, where there are any, will be expected to be doing all sorts of other things because the labour force on hill farms has been cut to the minimum. All too often it is now reduced to only the farmer himself.

Local sheep dog trials were the one relaxation that the old shepherds enjoyed, where they pitted their dog-handling ability against their neighbours. These trials were started by men whose everyday job was herding sheep, whereas now one sees any number of contestants in 'One Man and his Dog' who have never herded sheep for their livelihood. Don't get me wrong, I wish I had their ability to handle dogs, which is a gift that I don't have, and they give tremendous pleasure to countless townees who watch the show on T.V. However the viewers are not seeing the old sort of trials that we used to have that really tested a dog. Nowadays all the trials are on golf courses or similar smooth surfaces, but the original trials were a test of a dog's ability to shift sheep out of the sort of terrain on which one had to gather. I think the hill trial at Cairndow will be one of the last, if not the last, genuine hill trial in Scotland.

When I started the Lagganbridge Dog Trials back in the fifties I said I wanted them run on hill ground, and I was told all those forty years ago that the possible contestants wouldn't enter—and at that time these were people who made their living in herding sheep on hill land. People like the MacPhersons from Corrour, one of the wildest, roughest and wettest areas in the Highlands, where one would never get a sheep in a fank without good dogs. Andrew and his son, Raymond, who became an International Champion, roughed it in their house in Corrour miles from another human habitation, but they were always turned out immaculately at the trials. When they were away from home they left the dogs they didn't need at the trials in a barn with a deer hanging from the rafters on which they could do a self-service job. There was a 'boley hole' made in the door so that the dogs could go to the burn for water, as when they are being fed meat, their natural food, dogs drink a lot. I visited Corrour once when the Macs weren't at home, so I know that this is what happened: but although the dogs looked the picture of health and many went on to cover themselves with glory at dog trials, I have a feeling that some townees who cosset their beloved 'pooches' wouldn't approve.

I'll never forget my first Lagganbridge Trials, which I had organised to be run on a big haugh I had by the river Spey. This was surrounded by a floodbank which was ideal for spectators to sit on and watch the proceedings. As we were starting from scratch we needed money, so I went to all the local landlords asking for their support, telling them that the famous Jim Wilson was the judge and that he would give his famous demonstration of the figure of eight, i.e. three dogs lying down and his fourth putting the sheep round them. When Jim came to stay with me, with his super wife, Nell, who acted as secretary, he opened the boot of what he called his 'motor', which was a Jaguar. When I quizzed him as to why he chose that make of car he replied: 'Because there's enough room in the boot for four dogs'. But on the evening in question, to my consternation, only three came out. 'Jim,' I said, 'you're meant to be giving a demonstration of the figure of eight tomorrow, and I've got all the local lairds and their house parties coming specially to see you'. Jim replied: 'The fourth dog was a bitch, and she's in season. Never use a bitch for trials, Ben, they always let you down. I'll find something for you for tomorrow'.

I did not sleep easily that night, but was so busy next day organising gate-keepers, sheep, men to put the sheep out of the release pen, the man supplying the 'mike' (which was usually a disaster forty years ago) etc., etc., that I forgot about the demonstration until halfway through the morning. As it happened, an innkeeper from Speyside had a dog that had been trained by Jim at the trials. Like many more today, this person didn't have sheep but wanted to run a dog. His run was a disaster—the dog peed on the first mole-hill, chased the only brown hare ever seen on Gaskbeg and nearly put the sheep in the Spey before being called off. As the owner passed his 'motor', Jim said: 'Put him in the boot, Fachy'. I, as course director, suddenly real-ised what Jim was about to do. Stupidly I said to him: 'Jim, I've got the whole of the "crème de la crème" of the county here to see the famous Jim Wilson and his equally famous dogs, please don't make a fool of yourself'. The reply was brief: 'Ben, get on with your job as course director and I'll get on with mine'. Three o'clock came, the time advertised when one would see the one and only Jim Wilson etc., etc. and as I announced it Jim let the four dogs out of the boot of the motor. He took the red dog, 'Glen', which had made such a mess of his earlier run, by the scruff of the neck, shook him and said: 'It's me!' He then went to the starting pole, set his other three dogs down behind him to form the figure of eight, and sent Glen away to do one of the best outruns, lifts and fetches seen all day, as well as putting the sheep through the other three dogs. That's brilliance and a great gift.

Glen later was returned to Jim, who then very kindly gave him to me because he couldn't use him as a trial dog. The reason for this was that he would take the occasional grip of a sheep, just as he did with the wether on Ben Alder mentioned earlier. For someone wanting to catch a sheep this is most useful, but in dog trials is heavily penalised. Glen had a barrel chest, which gave him plenty of heart and lung space, and he could go all day. In the Laggan area he was known as the 'Sputnik', because he wanted to gather the whole hirsel on his own. Many a hill shepherd could do with his sort today.

Sadly, in this country of ours once known as the 'Stud Farm of the World', we have got too clever by half. Ayrshire cows were judged by the confor-mation of their bags, so that in the end there was more bag than the milk it should produce. Clydesdale horses had so many fancy things done to their feet and hocks that there was no way they could get into a tattie drill, and some would have found it hard to pull a cart. Aberdeen-Angus bulls were bred for the American market so small they could hardly bull a cow. Border collies were bred to 'keek', but in no way could they shift a bulk of sheep or the stubborn old ewe from behind that big stone. My fellow musketeers, like me, are delighted to see the countryside brought to the townees through T.V. programmes like 'One Man and His Dog', but the breeding of the sort of collie required for that specialised kind of trial has not done much good for the few shepherds still left gathering in vast areas of the Highlands. These Highland sheep farms are full of boulders and hidden ground that the handler can't see, but out of which a dog with some force can winkle the sheep.

I remember when I was lucky enough to be given a farm manager's job on my return from the war, I bought a dog for two pounds. It had been advertised in a paper (the vendor's first expense), sent to Perth from the Borders by train (second expense), where I collected him from the guards van where, in those days, one often found livestock (and the resultant smell of urine). Then the vendor wrote me a long letter (third expense), in which he said he was sure I would be well satisfied, as the dog would shift cattle or sheep—which he did really well—and that 'he would follow me like glue'. I think he got his metaphors a bit mixed up, but 'Mac' did stick to me like glue, and even swam the river Earn with me one night to bring back some cross-Highland bullocks that obviously thought my neighbour on the other side of the river had better grass than I was supplying.

Why is it that the cakes on the other table always look better than the ones on one's own table? I think it's one of the problems in our countryside today, when townees buy their 'shangri-la' in the country, and then spend their time moaning about the smell of dung, the cockerels crowing at dawn, the antiquated rural bus services and the fact they can't run 'Fifi' in a field that has ewes and lambs in it. Yet they only see the good side of our way of life on TV. or when they are on their summer holidays.

But back to August in a shepherd's year. Donald was saying that due to the size of the Ardkinglas Estate and the dicey weather one used to get in the west in July (and I say advisedly, used to get, because as I write in 1998 they have had a better spring and early summer than those of us in the east), often they weren't finished clipping in July and were still on the go in August. Sometimes the weather was so bad only half a hirsel might be gathered, and they had to do what we called a 'back gather', i.e. gather the hirsel a second time. This however was more common at the November gatherings for the winter dipping, when one wanted to have the numbers for the dreaded forms one had to fill in for the Department of Agriculture. Nowadays sheep owners love those returns because on them depends the headage subsidy they will get.

Donald was also saying he liked to have five good dogs, of which one had to be a 'hunter'. A hunter is a dog that does just that, hunts a bulk of sheep away from the shepherd, as opposed to a 'wearer' who brings the sheep to the shepherd. The old hunters were often 'beardie' collies, i.e. they were rough coated, and many I knew thirty to forty years ago were bred in Skye. Many, in fact most, had a good bark about them, which of course is not allowed in sheep dog trials.

The shepherds of Cairndow after a gather in 1968.

A STICK, HILL BOOTS AND A GOOD COLLIE DOG

What amazed me was that neither Donald or Pat ever got money for the keep of their dogs until the Wages Order came in. Even then, they said, without the odd dead sheep or venison—as both worked on Estates that had deer stocks, but many shepherds wouldn't have that advantage—they wouldn't have managed to keep their dogs in working trim on the amount allowed. It never ceases to amaze me how the Border collie, as it is now called, has become not only the champion of sheep dog trials worldwide, but is also the tops in agility tests and in finding stupid climbers who go out in the wrong climbing gear and in weather that real hill men would never venture out in. Yet these dogs are bred from a line that were but sparsely fed, is there a lesson there for us mere humans?

What a pity that, for a multitude of reasons, there is not the amount of grouse on our Highland hills there was in the thirties. Pat was saying how much money used to be poured into Perthshire during August. Although he was shepherding in August he was also out loading the second gun for a shooting tenant. One tenant had a train privately booked from Sussex to Scotland, which had on it cars and a workforce which consisted not only of butlers, chauffeurs and valets, but also of thirty ladies, much to the delight of the mainly male staff in Glenartney. This tenant used to supply a barrel of beer to the twice-weekly dances on Tuesdays and Fridays, which as you can imagine was 'manna from Heaven' for the young lads who were on the minimum of wages. The input to the local economy from mid-July until the 10th of October, the end of the deer-stalking season, was immense. I deliberately say deer stalking, as day after day when I open my paper at a heading about 'stalking' I think it's going to be about some deer-forest or other, only to find it's some love-lorn male following a female who is not as 'chancy' as he thought!

But not every shepherd in the old days was lucky enough to be on an estate that rented out a grouse moor, and as I've written most were probably fully taken up gathering for 'roughies', ewes that had missed the main July gatherings. So low were the wages then that the house cow made up a large part of them. As the cow's keep, hay, had to be made by the shepherd, it was usually August before he got round to the job. The 'coo pairk' was a tiny enclosure that had never seen nitrogen, and so the hay was meadow hay made up of lovely old grasses—weeds to many a younger farmer today. August, or at the earliest, the end of July, would be the time to cut it, and for all too many this was done by a scythe! I milked a house cow until I retired at the age of seventy, and admittedly for the last ten years I used a small milking machine. A lot of my neighbours laughed me to scorn as they said it was uneconomic and unhygienic. On the first count I would say, 'well, the cream Sally makes into butter, and it is super for porridge in winter and fruit in summer, we have lovely tasty milk, and the skim goes to the pigs that give us Scottish, naturally reared bacon, not like Danish bacon, a lot of which seems to be water and whatever other additives one wouldn't know.' On the score of hygiene, it is interesting that my daughter, when serving with the Save the Children Fund in Ethiopia (known as Abysinnia when I fought there all those fifty-seven years ago), was the only one not to get a tummy infection that all the other Brits got. When quizzed by the Medic as to where she was brought up—answer, on a farm in Scotland—the next question was, 'What milk did you drink?' Answer, 'Milk from the house cow that Dad hand-milked'. Medic's reply: 'You are a lucky lass—the result of that is, you have built up some antibodies'. That prompts me to ask whether, as a nation, are we getting too hygiene-conscious?

Things were very different in different parts of the country in August. While those shepherding the vast open tracts of country in the West Highlands were still trying to get all their 'roughies' gathered, those dependent on the grouse shooting had to have everything finished before the 'Glorious Twelfth'. Yet Pat was willing to admit that even then, when he went to help out at the grouse shooting, he always took a dog (one that was not gun-shy as many are) plus a pair of shears to get the odd 'roughie' that would come in front of the grouse beaters. Donald says that many a time when they were gathering sheep for the dog trials they would have a 'roughie' in the lot, and there would be a lot of banter as to which competitor would get her. These sheep, having skipped a gathering or two, were always wily old girls. When I ran at the trials I was surprised that, as factor of the estate, the 'roughie' wasn't included in my lot!

But all in all August was a month for clearing up at the end of the clipping period and getting ready for the shepherd's 'crown of the year' month, September, when all his year's work came to fruition. This was the month for the sale of his top wether lambs and his second draw ewe lambs, if he was lucky enough to be on a good enough farm to have spare ewe lambs to sell: naturally the best were kept for replacement stock. So let's look forward to September—to my mind, in the days when all one's stock was sold through the auction ring, the pinnacle of a shepherd's year.

September

I finished my August chapter by saying September was the crown of the year for a shepherd herding Blackfaced hill sheep. It was the month when, in the old days, all stock was sold through auction marts and the shepherd's whole year's work depended on 'the fall of the hammer'—the amount his lambs made when the auctioneer's hammer fell and the price was announced to the assembled throng, which fifty years ago was usually a packed auction mart. Nowadays there are few auction marts and many other outlets for the lambs: they end up being sold as dead weight, or through co-operatives, or direct to overseas markets etc.

What fun those old days were, with the crack, the drams and most of all the rivalry on big estates between shepherds on different hirsels or between farms. After all his year's work the shepherd had the great experience of being in the ring with 'his' lambs (and as an owner for a time I know only too well that a really good shepherd looks on his hirsel as 'his' and the lambs as 'his' lambs).

We in Scotland have the honour to have held the biggest one-day sheep sale in Europe, at Lairg in Sutherland, where in 1991, forty thousand were sold. MacDonald, Fraser and Co. started this sale back in 1894 when they set up some pens beside Lairg railway station. In those days all stock were moved by rail, as they continued to be well into the late nineteen-fifties. I remember when I was in Gaskbeg and managing the Cluny herd of Aberdeen-Angus, the bulls were always sent to Perth from Newtonmore by train, and the trains were first-class then with first-class rolling stock. Now all sheep from Lairg are transported in those vast lorries that were never meant for anything smaller than a motorway! Lairg will be one of the few marts where a few lots are still walked over the hills to the sale: sadly all too many of us today have lost the power of our legs, and transport everything, ourselves and our stock, by some sort of vehicle.

The Lairg sales were, and still are, for the famous North Country Cheviots or 'Northies' as they are affectionately called. Since many of that breed are bred on arable land in the counties of Ross and Cromarty, Caithness and Sutherland, the Lairg main sale is in August, not September when most Blackfaced lamb sales are held. Just as many wet west coast estates and farms were clipping in August when east coast places were long finished, so east coast lambs were ready for sale in August, not September. The Northies were introduced to the four northern counties by noted Border flockmasters who bred the South Country Cheviots in their native Border hills. I suppose due to the goodness of a lot of the land they graze they have grown bigger in their new environment. To this day there are well known Border families who have farms in the north, the Elliots being an outstanding example.

Roley Fraser, grandson of the founder of the Lairg Mart, said he always got a brace of grouse from a certain landowner if he made a decent job of selling her lambs, the Lairg sale being just after the Glorious Twelfth. But as I've said, auction marts are falling by the wayside, more's the pity. In the old days they were part of the patchwork of services that made up our agricultural communities, like our shops, post offices, churches and village halls—though sadly, in Scotland, not our pubs. At that time these were 'spit and sawdust' drinking howffs, but they are slowly becoming more congenial! In my time and in my district, Crieff, Glendevon, Auchterarder, Killin and Aberfeldy Marts have all gone to the wall, and with them the chance for an exchange of views and a chance for young stockmen to see each other's stock.

As for my fellow 'Musketeers', when Pat was in Lanarkshire his lambs were sold in Lanark, where his top wether lambs went one day and his mid-ewe lambs the next. The poorer or smaller ones went to Biggar (another mart under the shadow of closure as I write). Lanark then had an outstanding auctioneer in Ian Clark, who was more than good to me in my managing days because I had served in the war and he had wanted to go but was in a reserved occupation.

It's amazing the difference a good auctioneer can make to the price of a pen of lambs, and post-war I was lucky enough to know some of the tops—Ian Clark, Jim Craig (Ayr and Newton Stewart) and Lovat Fraser and his son Roley (Perth, Lairg and Cairndow) and now much later, David Leggat, but there must be many more. I remember once saying to Lovat what a gift he had of knowing the price a pen of lambs or a pedigree bull would make, and he replied: 'Ben, it's much better knowing who might buy them'. This may be the reason that when a soon-to-be well-fleeced Yank or Argentinian was bidding on a bull, I occasionally had a funny feeling that there was a fly on the wall waving a catalogue against the main bidder! But be this true or false, it would be impossible among a lot of hard-headed (and in many cases hard-hearted) farmers buying lambs. I say hard-hearted advisedly, because some had a bonanza during and immediately after the war when food was scarce and this country held its farmers in high regard, but later the same ones moaned like mad and wouldn't help the industry. I had my own experience of this. Because I had inherited a good voice from my father I was used in farming broadcasting, but as I wasn't a farmer's son I was shunned by many of the old school.

In those days there was a half hour farming programme on the radio every night with repeats in the morning, and I and other farmers were used on 'Matter of Opinion', the Scottish version of 'Any Questions'. But in this present year, 1998, with farming in the doldrums, there is only half an hour a week on farming matters. 'Landward', our Scottish farming programme on T.V., and an excellent one at that, has had to introduce all sorts of extra environmental material etc. and has had, I understand, a hard fight to survive.

What has this to do with the autumn sheep sales, I hear you say? Well, just this, that with agriculture seemingly not needed in Britain any more, as there are no longer the queues for food that I remember so well during and after the war, the arable farmers, who did so well for so many years, and who used to buy the hill lambs, no longer want them. What worries me is that the hills have in the past supplied the breeding stock for many of the top sheep and cattle units on our more fertile acres, and not only that, have

A modern Blackfaced ewe—compare her to the older type as shown in the picture later in the chapter.

supplied a lot of first-class stockmen and women: but both of those 'gushing springs', shall we call them, are about to dry up.

Donald, on the other hand, looked on Glasgow (now closed) and Dalmally (which has had a vast amount of money spent on it) as his local sales. My first experience of Dalmally was when I was managing Ben Challum Ltd. Estate (1947-51), which included Arrivain, now planted, between Tyndrum and Dalmally. George Menzies was my head shepherd for the two thousand ewe stock, and he had drawn the cast ewes. These were five years old and too old for the hill, but suitable to go to a low ground farm and be crossed by a Border Leicester tup to produce the popular grey-faced lamb. He dressed them all, i.e. clipped any tufts left on them after a none-too-competent shearer had done his best. Then he painted a red band on their horns, which certainly enhanced their appearance. The great day came (actually in October) and he and his sister—also one of the best workers with a knowledge of sheep it was my honour to employ—walked them to Dalmally, some seven miles. When he got to the mart the ewes were put in a pen, where, because of the incessant rain and the previous sales, there was mud up to the ewes' hocks and knees. By the time I arrived 'Geordie' was fizzing. So much so, that after he had the usual dram or two with his pals he told me to see Harry Fraser, Lovat's brother and the chairman of Speedies Co. who ran the mart, and tell him the Ben Challum ewes were not being sold because of the condition they were in. I have never felt so useless as a factor, after agreeing to this, as when I saw Geordie and his sister and friends literally pull every ewe out of the mud in the pen to be walked the seven miles back up the road to Arrivain! This was the incident that led to the concreting of the pens at Dalmally—so anyone who uses Dalmally now and happens to read this book can thank old Geordie for starting what has turned this mart on its head.

I wonder how many other businesses depended on two or three sales for their annual income as did farming in those days. Nowadays all too many farmers farm for what one hill farmer of my acquaintance called the 'Subsidey' (subsidy) which has not helped to maintain the standard of the stock for sale. When I went to Gaskbeg in 1951 the Kingussie Mart was run by my friends MacDonald and Fraser from Perth, but sadly they weren't willing to spend any money on the deteriorating pens. As the local N.F.U. Chairman I felt the area deserved better, especially the crofters of whom there were many. As a result we in the Badenoch Branch of the N.F.U. decided to form a co-operative, and as MacDonald and Fraser were not interested in getting involved, Aberdeen and Northern Marts came in and I'm proud to say it is going great guns to this day.

A pen of the older type of Blackfaced ewes at a sale (Polly Pullar).

A STICK, HILL BOOTS AND A GOOD COLLIE DOG

I always remember Lovat Fraser telling me that at one cast ewe sale in Kingussie (in October) it was snowing and also blowing a gale. The only shelter in the old mart before the Co-op was formed was above the tiny office. This consisted of a hut behind the auctioneer and a bit of corrugated iron above him, which on the day in question was no use at all as the wind was blowing off the Cairngorms which the auctioneer faced. When a pen of sheep is sold the auctioneer marks down the price and the purchaser on a piece of paper, and usually puts a dozen or so on a page before passing it back to the clerk in the office. In Kingussie the office had a wee 'boley hole' through which Lovat passed the slips, and there was a shutter to close it. Such was the severity of the storm that Lovat said he had to push the sale transaction 'line', as it's called, through the 'boley hole' after each pen was sold. Even then there was a miniature snowdrift on the desk on which he noted the sales and brought down that famous gavel. That gavel had clinched deals worth thousands of pounds (worth millions today) for Shorthorn and Aberdeen-Angus bulls in the forties and fifties, but also was used to equal effect to get a wee crofter the last bob or two for his few lambs.

Lovat Fraser, as I've already said, was one of the great auctioneers it has been my pleasure to see in action, and although he will be remembered (if there are any others left to remember him) as the person who sold all the expensive bulls to the States, Canada, Argentina etc. in the fifties, I will remember him in particular as someone who knew the value of sheep at the time of a sale, and so could put the bottom in a market that might otherwise have been a disaster.

Even a townee with no knowledge of the sheep trade, and I hope one or two reading these reminiscences will be of that ilk, will realise that those wee marts situated near the source of the input (lambs, ewes and suckled calves, mainly) depended on an honest auctioneer who knew the price of stock. Otherwise the wee farmers and crofters had to rely on the dealers, who sadly were all too often not as straight as they might have been. I have seen all too many times dealers buying stock from small farmers and crofters who have laboured all year to produce their few beasts. The dealers then have someone at the exit to the ring demanding, not asking for, a 'luckspenny'. This habit is to my mind terrible: it is meant to be the seller giving back to the buyer some money to give him 'luck' with his purchase, but has got completely out of control. It has now got to such an extent that I sometimes wonder how much 'luckspenny' passes after some of the huge prices paid for rams.

But as usual I've strayed from the sales in September. After we had formed the Co-op mart in Kingussie I was thrilled to be appointed manager of the Glentromie and Gaick Estates, part of which was the farm of Ruthven (the famous Barracks are on it). The wedder lambs from that farm topped the sale at six pounds per head, a lot of money in those days, and cause for all too much celebration at the nearby Silverford Hotel. Luckily this was in the days before the drink-driving laws were in being. Our cars, however, were so slow and there was so little traffic on the road that there were more accidents caused by stags jumping over cars and smashing windows than there were by vehicles hitting each other. History doesn't relate how many ancient vehicles with equally ancient drivers were pulled out of ditches after those lamb sales.

When I was appointed factor of the Ardkinglas Estate back in 1959 it had eight thousand breeding ewe stock. The selling of the resultant lambs, which, apart from the ewe lambs being kept for stock, would be in excess of four thousand, meant days away from the estate for myself and the shepherds, most of the time kicking our heels while waiting our turn in the catalogue. As I have stated it was the shepherd's big day in the year, or one of the very few they had in those days, as it was before most shepherds, especially the old and bold, had cars. As I always tried to get two hirsels of lambs to the sale, be they the tops, the seconds or the shotts, it meant that myself, two shepherds and the lorryman all had to be absent for a day from jobs we should have been doing back on the estate. Although I used to drive the lorry on occasions myself, this was not at all popular with its usual driver as he was not only responsible for its maintenance but also doubled as a tractor man. As he wasn't one of the world's hardest workers, although a delightful person, he would rather have had a day at a sale than one at home working.

As a member of the Royal Smithfield Show Council which runs the Fatstock Show in London each year, I had met a dynamic Welshman, one Captain Bennet Evans, with whom I got on extremely well, and blow me down if we weren't both appointed to the original Hill Farm Research Organisation under the late Arthur Wannop's chairmanship. This was when I was at Gaskbeg and before I went to Ardkinglas. At one of our evening unofficial sessions when the 'usquebaugh' was flowing (and more sense was being talked than had been all day!) Bennet Evans asked me about Kingussie Mart, how it was going etc., etc? Then he told me that he sold all his sheep actually on his farm, which was a large one for Wales, but from memory had only four thousand ewes compared with Ardkinglas's eight thousand. He described how he could show his sheep much better, as they hadn't been shoved on and off a lorry and driven for miles to a mart and so on. So with his advice in mind I suggested to my bosses John and Michael Noble that we should hold a similar sale at Cairndow.

I will never forget the traumas we had at the first sale, nor will one of the other 'Musketeers', Donald, who was head shepherd at the time. We had to plan the sale like a major army operation (although as a mere Sergeant-Major and later an officer I was never in a position to carry one out, I knew what it entailed). Firstly we had to fix a date between the usual lamb sale dates and the cast ewe dates, the former usually being in early September, the latter early October, and get auctioneers to agree to it. We settled for around the third week in September. Then we had to decide when we were going to gather, and which hirsel to gather first. We only had a certain amount of inbye fields: if we gathered too early we would overstock the fields and if we did it too late we'd miss the sale date. You can imagine the amount of work it entailed. It was a new idea, and it meant the shepherds wouldn't get their day away. Although the Glasgow market was a terrible dump and smelly, and well away from the shopping centre, the boys, natu-rally, liked to have their day away from home. Having said that, the shepherds gave me a great backing and we all discussed the best way to organise and run the sale.

At that time in the early sixties there was little traffic on the A83 over the Rest and Be Thankful on the stretch from Tarbet to Campbeltown via Cairndow, and the only sheltered accommodation (essential for buyers and auctioneer, even more so in Argyll with its rainfall) suitable for the sale, was at Clachan, now famous country-wide for its Oyster Bar. Most of the sheep, and as I've said there were over four thousand to be sold, had to be walked over the old bridge which spanned the River Fyne. Could you imagine trying to do that today? We had a terrible build-up to the sale as Argyll did its worst weather-wise, with constant mist on the hills, and I was a nervous wreck. But the shepherds were magnificent, and in the last week before the sale we operated two squads, one gathering a hirsel and the other sorting out the sheep into wether lambs, ewe lambs, shott lambs (the wee totie ones that wouldn't be saleable until much later) and the cast ewes, cast only for age and bought by arable farmers to cross with Border Leicester or similar tups to produce cross lambs. The ewes to be retained as the stock and the best of the ewe lambs for keeping up the stock were also sorted. Anyone who has not been in a fank actually doing the job would find it hard to imagine how time-consuming it can be, and for Donald and his squad it must have been traumatic. I've no doubt that 'Captain Ben' was not the most popular man in Argyll during that week!

I meantime had to liaise with auctioneers, caterers (as food and drink are essential at any sale) the estate workers who had to erect pens all around the old Clachan steading, and, most important of all, the buyers. Forest Smith, now sadly gone, was one of the top sheep dealers in the country. He had always bought some lambs from Ardkinglas, and he not only came but brought some friends with him who also bought. The fact that it was the first sale of its kind in Scotland and that Michael Noble was Secretary of State engendered a lot of interest and the sale was a rip-roaring success. The only real problem I had on sale morning was that the auctioneer from Glasgow kicked up hell because his clerk (a rather good-looking blonde) was feeling cold in the site I had designated as the auctioneer's office and could I find a stove? Eventually I got an old paraffin stove for them, but I had a strong feeling that the good-looking clerkess was more used to being warmed by the auctioneer, judging by the fuss he made. After this super sale, of course in true West Highland style we went to celebrate in the Cairndow pub afterwards. There Alastair MacCallum, now a head shepherd but then a junior, gallantly stood a round of drinks as his hirsel had sold so well, only to find that the round cost him his week's wages. I have found shepherds a most generous lot of folk, changed days indeed. Everyone has their 'very good years', as the late Frank Sinatra sings of the different stages in his love life, and for me bringing off that sale at Cairndow must make that year one of my best.

As for the month of September, together with October it is 'top of the pops' for me. It's the fruition of a year's work. Oh, I know the 'nights are drawing in' as my old Dad used to say, much to my mother's annoyance, but I always felt when I was farming on my own account, or managing estates for others, that September and October proved whether or not one had done a good job that year. Everything one had produced off the soil, be it livestock or crop, was sold in those months, and the prices gained told one whether one was any damned good or not. The colours in our Scottish countryside are taking on that lovely tint that in my many travels overseas I have only seen rivalled by Canada in the fall (though the Canadian-Scots I met said they would rather have our autumn than their fall). But by the end of September the shepherds were starting to think about their plans for next year.

October

October to me has always been a magical month. Oh, I know the nights are drawing in, but I love the colours one gets in that month and the crispness that usually goes with them. Where better to see these colours than on our hills with the bracken (of which there is far too much) and the rowans down by the burns? Generally the feeling I have is of a year that has gone but with a wish to savour what's left of it and hope next year will be even better. The good book promised us a seed time and a harvest, and in the fifty years that the 'Three Musketeers' have been working with sheep that promise has always been fulfilled, with some years better than others. And for a hill man preparation for the next year's seed time starts with the buying of the tups who will plant the seed in the ewes for the next year's lamb crop and subsequent harvest.

How the Tup Sales have changed over the last half century. The dates are the same, with Stirling in the first week of October, followed by Newton Stewart and Perth and then Lanark in mid-October. These were for the Blackfaced breed of sheep, which are still the most numerous in Britain. In the old days there was a very big difference between the types of sheep sold at those Tup Sales. Perth always went for the heavier-woolled but lengthy sheep. Newton Stewart catered for the short-woolled sheep which were shorter in the back but left milkier females. Lanark in those old days had the top-priced tups bred by some of the top sheep men in the country. These produced a type half way between the Perth and what were called the 'bare-skinned' type favoured in the south west. As I have already written Ian Clark ruled the roost there in Lanark and the top prices for the Blackfaced breed were made in his mart.

To this day the tups in Lanark are making the news, with one sold in 1997 for eighty-five thousand pounds by old friends of mine, the McCall-Smiths at Connachan in the Sma' Glen, whom I have known since my days at Millhills in the late forties. I'm afraid I can never understand a sheep, without a pedigree (or even with one) making that price. Just imagine yourself, as I used to be, in a hill farm one thousand feet above sea level and battling against the elements that that sort of farm encounters, and you are looking to the man from the Ministry of Agriculture to help you as best he can with a hill sheep subsidy. He very rightly says, 'but some of your lot can afford eighty-five thousand pounds for one sheep, so you can't be as hard up as you make out you are'.

Even more annoying to me as an oldie is how the tup trade is governed by 'fads' just like ladies' fashions. Fifty years ago the tups all had to have 'a bell on their broo', a white mark resembling a bell on their black brow. And the horns had to be set in a certain direction like the ones in the picture at the beginning of this chapter. Imagine my surprise, not having been in contact with the breed for some time, to see so-called Blackfaced sheep at Braco and Dalmally shows that looked more like Swaledales. This breed, until just after the war, was totally unknown in Scotland.

Back in 1948 I was sent by Duncan Stewart, that great stocksman and my then boss, to go to Kirkby Stephen to buy five Swaledale tups, as he had heard that they were great snow breakers. At that time on Ben Challum on the estate of that name we had a hirsel of three year old wethers.

My Ford van in those days had no proper division to keep the resultant purchases from breathing down my neck! There was no M-road or even the half decent A74 in those far off days and it took a helluva long time to go and get back, but I do remember the average price for the five was five pounds and they included the reserve champion! What I remember even more vividly was the reception I got at the next N.F.U. meeting, when I got stick for introducing this foreign breed to the Highlands! But nowadays,

This tup made one of the top prices in 1998. Compare it with the drawing of the older type of tup at the beginning of this chapter.

judging by the sheep I have seen recently at the two shows I've mentioned, some people have used more than the first cross, and as for the old 'Blackie' horn that gave so much character to a sheep's face, they now seem to want it shaped like the handle-bars of the four-wheeled motorbikes they all ride!

But wherever one farmed or shepherded in the hills, the tup sales were great occasions, as of course were all sales as we didn't move around then as we do now. Pat used to have to bring back tups from Lanark for neighbours as well as those bought by his boss. He found the best thing to do with them was shut them in a shed fairly tight so that they hadn't room to take a race at each other, as with enough space to manoeuvre their charge can break their opponent's neck, and as they all go by smell they know the tups that have come off other farms. During the time Donald and I worked together at Ardkinglas, when I brought the tups home we got the shepherds together, and after the toss of a coin they would take turns in choosing a tup for their hirsel. Where possible I tried to swap ram lambs from one hirsel to another, as sheep that are acclimatised to a certain area, especially in a tick-infested district, are so much more use than ones that have probably been overfed and have been brought up on arable ground—the ones Duncan Stewart said fell into ditches because they thought they were troughs! Newton Stewart tups just after the war were largely brought out with a minimum of feed, and between 1947 and '51 I used to go there to buy thirty or more tups for Ben Challum. The prices then were about five pounds a head, and many a good tup I bought out of the pen reserved for Armstrong the dealer whose rams were destined for the killing house, as I had to fill the railway wagon that was to take them to Killin station (now Beechinged and sadly missed).

James Craig, already mentioned, sold for the whole two days, and always had a wee bit of pawky humour which so helps to lift a sale. As pay was low for shepherds in those days it was usual for a good employer to give his shepherd a tup lamb. I remember a wee shepherd coming in with his tup lamb and Jim saying: 'Now you must help this wee man as he has a big family'. Then there's a story I've told before. After I had left Ben Challum and gone to farm on my own at Gaskbeg I had become friendly with the Wilson brothers—Jim, the doyen of sheep dog handlers with nine international wins, and Ben from Troloss who was the tops at bringing out tup lambs in Lanark. It was the period when those who usually consigned to Lanark realised that Newton Stewart was on the up and up and might take over. So Ben Wilson asked me to buy a certain tup lamb for him at Newton Stewart but in my name, which I did. Next year when I went back and was buying for myself, Jim knocked the lamb down and added, 'Is that for Ben Challum,

Ben Coutts or Ben Wilson?' Very quick, I thought. Later on there were sales like Oban, Dalmally, Fort William, Inverness, Biggar etc., mainly aimed at those buyers who had nowhere to put their tups—which all too often have been known to get out with ewes before they were meant to.

Quite the best after-dinner speech I've ever heard, and I've heard all too many long dreary ones, was given by a well known tup breeder back in the early fifties. The occasion was the annual dinner of the Argyll area N.F.U. in Oban. Michael Noble, at a time before he was an M.P., far less Secretary of State for Scotland or Lord Glenkinglas, was President of the area N.F.U. At that stage I was in Gaskbeg and Vice President of the Highland Cattle Society, and he asked me to propose the main toast to the area. Believe it or not there were eight speakers in all, and some, not me I'm glad to say, were extremely verbose! The last speaker, who was to reply to the toast 'To the Blackfaced Breed of Sheep', was this well known tup breeder. The time was now past midnight and he had dined 'extremely well'. He was a first class stocksman, who had pulled himself up by his bootlaces from shepherding, through managing, to tenanting a good farm. However he was known to feed his tups heavily and not in an appropriate way for the hard wet places where they all too often landed up. In the case of his tups this was the west of Scotland, as he had influence with the livestock inspectors in the Department of Agriculture who bought tups for the Islands. In fact once in Oban he had fourteen tups, of which thirteen were bought by the D.O.A.S. As a wise old 'Mulach' (man from Mull) said to the Department employee: 'And what was wrong with the fourteenth?' Anyway, this well-known character got to his feet, helped by his neighbour, and gave the following speech: 'The Blackfaced breed are the greatest breed God ever made. They would need to be when you think what I've done to them!' He then slipped under the table very fu'! Brilliant, short, humorous and to the point. Oh, if only all after-dinner speeches were so!

Then of course in October there were the cast ewe sales. I always think these sales should be called the draft ewe sales, as the old girls have done their stuff on the hard hills but are still fit to do another breeding season on arable land with the resultant better feeding. Most hill farms cast their ewes at five-year-old but some keep them until they are six. In the old days a hill farmer's ability was measured on how good his cast ewes were and the price they made, with the result that a tremendous amount of effort was put into preparing them for sale. They were carefully trimmed of any tufts of wool left after the main shearing (all too easy to miss, believe me) and there was always a ring of red paint put on the horn, which I must say greatly enhanced

Some medium-coated tups in a modern wood and metal fank (Polly Pullar).

their appearance. And if there was a speck of black in the fleece, that ewe would have no chance of being in the top drawer!

These were the old days when wool was wanted, partly because, as I've said before, there had been a war. Nowadays, I'm told, it costs more to shear sheep than one gets for the wool. Are we going back to the days that I recall, when one farmer I knew had two years' clip stored in his shed, as it was only worth two pence a pound!

The cast ewe sales in Perth in the fifties were a sight I'll never forget, when all the sheep men from the hills of East Perthshire and Angus congregated together to view and evaluate, and all too often to criticise, ewes from their neighbours' stock.

Geordie Menzies, as already mentioned, was my shepherd in Gaskbeg and took his only (and very short) holiday during the Perth ewe sales. Our ewes went to Kingussie as they weren't out of the top drawer. Geordie, however, had started his shepherding life at Urlar, Aberfeldy, which in his early days was one of the top tup-breeding flocks in that area. They depended on the price paid for their ewes at the Perth Sales as to how good their stock was thought to be, and to his dying day Geordie went to those sales. He used to leave Gaskbeg with up to twenty beautifully-made shepherds' crooks which he had spent all winter making. He did this with none of the modern electrical appliances I understand are used now, all he had was boiling water for getting the horn straight and then a 'rasp' (a file) and a knife to use while the horn was hot. He was a craftsman, and I regret now I have but one of his sticks left.

What amazes me today is to see the prices being paid for crooks which take a quarter of the time to make that Geordie's did. All he got were drams and a very few quid for those he took to the sales, but as he once said to me: 'Captain, it's my hobby and it fills in the long winter nights'. This after I said he ought to charge for his time. I have been honoured to judge the sticks at the Royal Highland Show not once but twice, and since then have seen many sticks for sale at agricultural shows, three day events etc. Seeing the prices asked now I wish Geordie and his like, who spent those long winter nights with their 'rasps', had lived to benefit from their craftsmanship, as many of their sticks would make monkeys out of some of the modern ones.

I must admit though that they had better horns to work with. In their day the tups, from which the horns were procured, weren't fed so hard, and the horns themselves were harder as a result. Now all too many are 'boss' (empty) in the centre and therefore useless for the job. This has become such a serious a problem for some stickmakers that they have given up using horn from Blackfaced rams and have turned to all sorts of horn from other breeds. Some makers are making lovely sticks out of the 'burr' of the wood, and I have one I cherish made by Hugh Boa in Mull, who is the first to admit he learnt a lot of his trade from Alastair Campbell, the last of a very distinguished stick-making family. Alastair's father won the championship at the Highland Show for his sticks more times than I can remember. The lovely thing about that family is that their craftsmanship is being passed on. Alastair, whom the grim reaper took from us last year, far too soon, had among many other good things he did for Mull formed a stickmakers class, and I've judged some excellent sticks that his students have made.

Stone dyking is also coming back when it was almost dying out. Oh, how I wish a Government would realise that these kinds of crafts stemmed from the work of hill farms, where we needed a good crook to catch a sheep and a good stone dyke to hold the flock for shearing, dipping, speaning etc., etc. Unless they encourage hill farming, the right-to-roam merchants and the ramblers will find they can't move for bracken, brambles etc. and even wolves, if some weirdies get their way.

But back to October and the ewe sales. When I was at Millhills in the late forties to early fifties and was looking after the ewe stocks of Balmuick and Brae of Fordie in Comrie and the Ben Challum Estate at Killin, I was never part of the elite who sold their cast ewes in Perth. Most of the Comrie ewes were brought down to Millhills to be put to a Border Leicester ram to produce grey-faced lambs, and the Ben Challum ewes went to Stirling and Dalmally. However I had three lovely friends who sold their ewes in Perth, all sadly no longer with us: they were Geordie Scott of Corriemuchloch, who managed for Sir William Rootes, the car magnate, who then owned Glenalmond Estate; Alastair Duncan-Millar, of Millar Remony on Loch Tayside, who made a marvellous job of showing how a Highland estate should be run (and I wish he was still with us to rebut the nonsense talked about 'wicked landlords'); and Brigadier Whitaker of Auchnafree in the Sma' Glen. The Brigadier was one of the hardiest men I knew and was seldom seen wearing anything more than his khaki shorts, even in the terrible winter of 1947. In the course of this he walked along the wind-swept tops of the Auchnafree hills to visit his friend Geordie Scott when he was seriously ill and the Brigadier's glen road was blocked feet deep.

Well, these three worthies had an annual tryst at the 'Foulford Inn', known locally as 'Johnnie Gorries', after the annual Perth cast ewe sale. They very kindly invited me to join them for the five years I was at Millhills, and if journalism had been allowed to print then what it does today after all those fifty-plus years, some flockmasters' ears would have been burning. The sale catalogue was brought out, the prices were scanned, the drams kept coming up and the discussion raged as to why so-and-so had sacked or employed a certain shepherd. We would be there for hours, but all I can say to the three departed is thanks, for all that I learned from you about farms, their owners and their shepherds. However I don't think you'd be too enamoured of the way the breed is going today. Among the things I learnt at one of these meetings was that there were farms to let north of the Highland Line with much less rent to pay than one had to in the Perth or Angus hills. That's how it came about that I got Gaskbeg, Lagganbridge, at the head of the Spey, although I had the chance of renting not one but two farms in Perthshire.

But as with many things in this country hill farms are judged much more by the price their tups make or, if they don't breed tups then by how much they pay for them. Pat, Donald and I all agreed we liked to see the ewe that produced the tup we fancied—easy for Pat in Lanarkshire but not for those of us looking after vast numbers of ewes on Highland estates that weren't established tup breeding units. That's the reason why I used to pick, with the shepherds, ram lambs out of good ewes from one hirsel and swap them with lambs from another hirsel. Another thing I did when at Ardkinglas, with Donald's full backing, was to buy ram lambs from a well known rambreeding stock that would have been castrated had we not bought them. After all they were bred the same way as the ram lambs that were being sold for prices that were outwith a commercial sheep farmers' budget. Donald very kindly said it made a huge difference to the Ardkinglas stock when I bought a lorry load of ram lambs from Jim Wilson, the famous dog handler and tup breeder at Whitehope, Innerleithen. From these we got a stock of ewe lambs all bred the same way, and looking the same, instead of a lot bred by tups from different breeders and not in any way uniform.

October was the month when the ewe lambs that were to be kept to keep up the stock (remember we were casting the ewes at five years old), had to be sent away to winter. This is (a) so that they were away from the possibility of being tupped (b) to allow them to grow more on better and cleaner keep, but most importantly (c) to relieve the sparse grazing that exists on the average Highland hill so that the ewes got what was available. All sorts of different areas were known as 'hogg wintering' areas, and in my time Speyside was the tops. Its great advantage back in the fifties was that there were no resident sheep flocks there, so the ground was clean, and the area is dry compared with the average high hill land that the hoggs came from.

Fifty years ago, when there were many more stocks of Blackfaced ewes than there are today, there were special trains laid on to take the hoggs to the wintering. These set off from Dalnaspidal, at the head of the Drummochter pass on the border between Perthshire and Inverness-shire. Here there was a special siding built for the hoggs coming from Loch Tayside, Glen Lyon and Glen Lochay, as well as those from the hill farms on Strath Tay which were driven over the hills to Dalnaspidal to be entrained for Morayshire. Geordie Menzies used to wax eloquent about having one helluva job getting the hoggs away from Urlar and over the moor, but when they came back in March they almost ran home.

One of my happiest duties when managing Ben Challum was driving Duncan Stewart, my boss, to book the winterings for the Ben Challum hoggs. The first stop was old Angus Gordon, at Finlarig near Dulnain Bridge. He was a well kent Aberdeen-Angus breeder of the old type of Speyside bulls that did so much to enhance the name of Scottish beef, but which in the end were to be ruined by some so called 'master breeders' who were pandering to the mighty dollar. Angus's first remark after welcoming us never varied: 'Whaur's the bottle, Mr. Stewart?' I was despatched to get a bottle of 'McCallum's Perfection' or 'Antiquary', both of which blends Duncan's family owned or had large shares in. Angus would then phone round his friends and relations, some of whom Duncan already knew, to tell them what the going rate was to be for the cost of wintering a hogg. Then the haggling would start. Angus had three sons and a daughter with whom we dealt. Alec, Jimmie and John, the sons, were all first class stocksmen who brought out suckled calves as only Speyside men could in those days, but the daughter was a tough cookie when it came to striking a bargain. We were talking in old pence in these days, and I remember well one day she was stirring the soup on an old black range with her back to Duncan and saying: 'Na, na, Mr Stewart, we'll need anither thripence'. And D.M., like all us mere males, gave in. That year the wintering was the worst we took, as the farm got flooded by the Spey and we lost, if I remember correctly, ten hoggs in the farm's ditches. This was because the hoggs hadn't been turned off the haughs onto the higher ground, which they should have been.

But every time I go up the new A9 and approach the Sloch summit and look left at a deserted croft with its demolished cottage, I think of the only time Duncan Stewart and I had words. We had been sent up there by a farmer in Nethybridge who said the crofter was a decent chap but needed some cash, the reason being that unless one has another job there is no way one can make a livelihood up there at twelve hundred feet above sea level, and at that time there was no 'service industry'. We were welcomed in and offered a seat around the open peat fire, seats which were cement bags that had been left in the rain and so become solid. Our tea was served in cracked mugs but the oatcakes were braw! Duncan beat the man down from five shillings and threepence apiece for wintering the hoggs to five shillings, and when we got outside I exploded. Whereupon Duncan said, almost sheepishly, 'I didn't want to do the man, I just love to haggle. Away back and offer him five shillings and sixpence'. I never carried out an order more cheerfully!

A postscript about McCallum's whisky: Duncan's first class stocksman, John Gordon, one of a family imported by Duncan's family from the north, used to say after having had a dram or two of his boss's own blend: 'The McCallum clan had as their battle cry "McCallum Mhor", but I say "More McCallum"!'.

November/December

No sun, no moon, no stars, November! But for all that, to those of us in hill sheep farms it was the beginning of the new year, as it was the month when the tups were put to the hill to mate with the ewes.

For me personally there are three days in November back in 1934 that I'll never forget to my dying day, when I visited the shepherds' meet in Mardale. In the summer of 1933 father had taken us on holiday to his favourite area of Britain, the Lake District, where he had been brought up and which was then completely unspoilt. As a climbing enthusiast he chose the Dun Bull Hotel at Mardale, since it was surrounded by nice climbable hills like Kirsty Pike, where he could start to teach the younger members of his brood of six to enjoy climbing.

I remember him telling me years later that Mr Daffern, the proprietor, charged him one old pound a week per head, and on this we lived like lords with nearly every meal home produced. Herdwick and Swaledale sheep were the native breeds that fed on the local hirsels. The Herdwicks were known for producing 'the King's mutton'—I know not which king this referred to, but he certainly knew his food as Herdwick mutton is superb. So we had that and their Aylesbury duckling which I'll never forget, although it's sixty five years ago! And of course all the vegetables were grown in their garden.

A STICK, HILL BOOTS AND A GOOD COLLIE DOG

Sadly the 'Dun Bull', the photo of which you see opposite, is no more. Nor have the farms Chapelhill, Flakhowe etc. survived, as they were all bulldozed and submerged to make way for the new Haweswater Reservoir, created to feed Manchester's needs for more water. But when I stayed there, as usual on all my schoolboy holidays, I went out and helped local farmers. Those around Mardale were some of the best of the many hill men it has been my pleasure to meet. Since those schoolboy days I've been honoured with two Nuffield Scholarships, one to the States in 1959 and another to Australia, New Zealand and South Africa in 1964. Through these I have met some of the world's top stocksmen, but now that I am eighty-two and looking back, to me the hill men of this country that I've met have been the tops. Those I met all those years ago are in that category. I must admit that as a hungry student (which I was at that time) the food provided at their handlings certainly helped, especially their apple tarts, but even without all that we got on first rate. To such an extent, in fact, that one of the famous Renwick family who have shepherded the Cumbrian and Westmoreland hills for generations said to me: 'You must come to the Mardale Shepherds' Meet in November'.

For the life of me I can't think how Dad, a stickler for schooling, let me off my studies, as just then I had failed my entrance exam to Vet. College and was being tutored. Nor do I know where the money came from to let me go. Now, however, I will be one of the few still left who can remember attending the famous 'Mardale Meets'. The background to these was that at the 'Dun Bull' they erected sheep pens where all the shepherds brought their 'stragglers'. These were sheep which didn't belong to them that had strayed on to their hill from their neighbours' farms. This was followed by a 'meet' of the Ullswater Foxhounds under the mastership of the one and only Joe Bowman, who is revered to this day as one of the greatest Fell huntsmen of all time.

The Ullswater pack were 'trencher fed' in the summer, i.e. each hound would go to a different home and be fed but would return in late August to be formed into a pack of hounds by Joe. 'Melville' was the hound that the 'Dun Bull' was feeding, but judging by the photograph I have of him I don't think he would fit into a modern Fell pack. The form was that shepherds came with their 'stragglers' and put them in pens marked for each neighbour's farm. Then, after a 'refresh' from the delightful Mr Daffern, they hunted the Fells with the Ullswater pack, all wearing their tackity boots turned up at the front for ease of movement going uphill. To this day I can tell an ex-shepherd or an ex-ploughman apart by their walk, since they have

The Dun Bull, Mardale. Now, sadly, no more.

completely different strides. As the old saying goes, never employ 'a galloping shepherd or a slow-moving ploughman'.

After their day's hunting, and what a super job those Fell packs do in controlling the hill foxes, some shepherds took their sheep and went home, but the majority stayed the night. I wondered, as a mere teetotal laddie, why I had been told to spread straw out in the barn. After the evening's carousel I learned the reason, as many of the shepherds just dossed down in the barn. It was that night all those years ago that I learned the words of 'Do you ken John Peel, with his coat so grey...' as we brought the rafters down, or nearly did. We should have done, had we known what bulldozers were going to do to the place later.

The next morning the shepherds, like all of their superb breed, were up at daylight, fed their collies, ducked their heads in the horse trough and then set off back to their farms. How I wish I had been older and able to take in more fully that I was participating in something that is now history. Nowadays I understand the Fell packs are followed by all too many cars, blocking roads that were never meant for vehicles, and very few actually follow the hounds as I did, on foot.

The Highland shepherds had no such excitement getting their stragglers home in the days before land-rovers and trailers. They simply made a tryst with their neighbour to meet on the march (boundary) between the farms where their stragglers were swapped. Nowadays the sheep are left in a fank, the neighbour is 'phoned and he goes round with his transport to collect them. Such is the shortage of labour today and the rate we live at, that sometimes the shepherds concerned never even see each other.

Once the ewes are all home and hefted the shepherd turns his attention to his tups. As they won't be doing much grazing for the five to six weeks they will be with their ewes, he will be feeding them. It amazes me, as it does my two 'advisers', how many sheep troughs are nowadays left in the same spot and not turned over. Not only does the ground round about them get fouled, leading to foot rot, but troughs left up attract seagulls, crows and jackdaws, and who knows what rubbish they were last eating or what disease they could be carrying. Pat says he always had a hoe with him with which he scraped out the troughs.

The ewes are all dipped to kill the 'beasties', and in the old days the shepherds thought that by doing this they were waterproofing them for the winter. Even as late as when we 'three musketeers' were boys, whale oil was added to the top of the tank full of dip, but it was actually useless. Previous to that, back in the last century, they used to 'smear' the sheep, with a mixture of eighty per cent tar and twenty per cent butter. For this purpose they had special smearing sheds, with a fireplace where the tar in pots was melted. The last and only one of these sheds I've seen is at Pole Farm, Lochgoilhead, with which Ardkinglas neighboured. As you see in the photo in this chapter the shed door was surmounted by a ram's head. Sadly I, and the tenant of the farm, Jim Jackson, can't make out the date underneath the ram's head. What a time it must have taken to slabber on that sticky mixture, and what a waste of good butter! The butter had to be added to keep the tar from completely gluing the wool together. When one thinks of the length of wool grown on the sheep in those days, and how every layer of wool had to be carefully folded over, smeared and then ditto with the next layer, even with the huge labour force they had in those days it must have taken weeks to 'smear' a hirsel, perish the thought.

Then too, the tups were so long coated that many had to have the ends of their fleeces trimmed in case the wool got balled up in the snow which was expected during November and December. The long woolled tups were still in vogue when Pat and Donald started shepherding as boys in the late twenties and early thirties—both have trimmed the fleeces, and in some cases even the bellies of tups. When the tups were put to the ewes depended where the farm was situated, in Lanarkshire Pat put them out on November seventeenth. On Ardkinglas, on the in-bye hirsels, they would go out on the twenty eighth of that month, but on the far out hirsels it would be the first of December.

Shepherds don't mind a bit of snow on the tops at 'tupping', they call it the 'white dog' since it keeps the ewes on the lower part of the hill. When I was talking about this to Ernie MacPherson, Donald's son, he was telling me, rightly to my mind, that he thought on those large units where you need three acres to a ewe, a shepherd could do more good at tupping time by keeping batches of ewes around the tup than he could at the lambing. If the ewes weren't tupped there wouldn't be any lambs!

When we all started there was a terrific amount of keel plastered onto tups but one doesn't see so much applied now. This was done so that the shepherds could easily make out where the tup was, and as some hills are fairly inaccessible this made sense. I know I've seen them in the Pass of Brander, Loch Awe, where they looked like some new red-coated breed of sheep. But it's all change now, and fences have been erected to make parks in which the ewes are kept at tupping time. Now, before lambing, ewes are scanned to see which are bearing twins, and those that are, are given special attention and often fed. Those that are not in lamb can be chucked out to

The ram's head over the door of one of the last of the old smearing sheds, at Pole Farm, Lochgoilhead, now tenanted by Jim Jackson (on the right).

the hill, if not out of the flock entirely. What a pleasant change from the days when we used to udder luck them, pressing our fingers into their tummies to see if there was a lamb there, which was crude to say the least and not exactly foolproof.

The number of tups put out on a hirsel depends on the district, but usually it's about three to the hundred. Some places liked to vary the ages of sheep they let out. Pat, when he was herding four hundred ewes on a well known tup breeding farm, put out one old sheep, two shearlings and two tup lambs. There the sale of tup lambs was the aim, and the second draw of ewe lambs would also command a good price.

Some shepherds swear by tup lambs as they think them more virile. I knew of one that got out for one day and a night and left fifty lambs, certainly some were twins, but what a man! But others weren't so keen. A tup was bought for Pat by one of his employers, but to Pat's fury the brute did nothing but sleep on a big stone in the middle of his hirsel and showed no interest whatsoever in his harem. At the end of tupping time Pat asked his boss to take him away, and the tup was consigned to the tup sale in Oban the following year. Oban at that time was looked on as the tup sale where one put one's secondary tups—ones which, in my humble opinion, could have been called rubbish even thirty years ago. Imagine Pat's feelings when he heard an acquaintance of his had bought it. The following spring Pat fearfully enquired how the tup had fared, and nearly fainted when told that he had left sixty nine lambs out of seventy ewes! I didn't know they had 'Viagra' thirty years ago!

As Ernie said, tupping time was more important on those wide Highland hills than lambing time, so December was the month when the shepherds were constantly on the hill and often met their neighbours on the tops. One of the neighbours of Alastair, the present head shepherd at Ardkinglas, was a man who was well known in the district, had been a good shinty player and a first-class judge of cattle, but like the rest of us had his faults. When he died there was a terrific turn-out, but the person giving the appreciation went over the top and you would have thought they were burying a saint! Alastair, as a near neighbour, was chosen to be one of the pallbearers who were asked to carry the coffin for a good half mile from the church. As they progressed up the street the coffin seemed to get heavier and heavier. Since the pallbearers knew the deceased wasn't a big heavy man, and also that he hadn't been, unlike the character described in the appreciation, as white as the driven snow, the man on the other side of the coffin to Alastair turned his head and remarked in a loud whisper: 'I think we've got the wrong man in the box, Alastair!'

A STICK, HILL BOOTS AND A GOOD COLLIE DOG

Looking back to the old days, one of the biggest changes we three have seen in the last fifty years is that the weather pattern has altered dramatically. We all remember the extreme weather of 1947 for varying reasons, but Pat recalls being out in shorts stalking with Fisher Ferguson on 6 September 1934, when six inches of snow fell and they had a job getting back to the game larder.

Then there has been the fantastic growth in research in sheep diseases, and no longer are worms and liver fluke etc. the plagues they were. I can't remember when I last saw a sheep with 'sturdy', a nasty wee worm that bored a hole in the sheep's head and had to be extracted with a small imple-ment like a corkscrew. Another development is those modern sheep fanks that make sheep handling so easy—no longer, thanks to the new designs, does one have to yank ewes by the horns to the dipper. Then there are those new dipping and in-wintering sheds, four wheeled motor bikes etc., etc. and I could go on. Yet despite these improvements, and although a shep-herd's pay has risen dramatically over the years, it still isn't an attractive enough life for most of the young people. Now too few of those reared among sheep want to work with them: many of the young shepherds of today come from other backgrounds, and are expected to do much more than look after a hirsel of ewes.

Donald, as I've recounted, was paid by cheque every six months back in the early thirties. After having slaved, for that's what it was back then, for half a year, imagine his feelings when he went to the bank to cash his cheque, having bicycled fourteen miles, to be told by the bank manager that Donald's boss had nothing in his account and so the cheque couldn't be honoured! However Donald stuck at the job and went on to become, not only a first-class shepherd who got his B.E.M., but also a well known shinty player. As an illustration of how things have altered financially since the old days, he told me of an incident after he had joined the Ardkinglas team of fifteen shepherds. He had an extra good dog, and the head shepherd said to him: 'I fancy that dog you've got and I could do with him, how much do you want for him?' Without waiting for a reply he went on, 'I'll let you know in the morning what I'll give you'. As they were in the middle of the summer gatherings, the next morning they were having a communal breakfast at a shepherd's house when the head man laid a single ten shilling note on the table, saying: 'That's for your dog, Donald'. A similar dog would be worth thousands today, but that's how much shepherding has changed over the last fifty years. And Pat's story of the mammoth clipping at the 'Are' shows the same thing, when they clipped four thousand ewes in one day and he was gathering ewes for days on end. One night he only got two hours sleep, but who would do that today? These are only two examples of the big changes in shepherding in the last fifty years.

When I asked my two mates what they did in December, apart from making sure that the tups were with the ewes, they replied in unison, 'As little as possible!' since it was one of their quietest months.

While I was in Sussex, Christmas was observed. Most of the shepherds there were, shall we say, believers: not bible-thumpers, but they acknowledged that all the things that meant so much to them—the changing seasons, the birds, the growth of the crops they needed to sustain their flocks, the birth of lambs and all the rest—were not man-made. They seldom got time to go to church, but as believers they made a point of being present at one of the many services that were on at Christmas. But the Church of England has always made more of the religious festivals than has the dour old Church of Scotland (of which I have been a member for sixty-five years and an elder for fifty of them). I was always annoyed that we in Scotland were expected to work on Christmas Day, but that the pagan festival of New Year was a holiday. But things have changed dramatically in the last fifty years, and now the whole country seems to shut down for the ten days covering Christmas and New Year. One stocksman I was talking to recently told me that when he fed the beasts that were in his care on Christmas Eve he gave them enough feed to last for two days, changed times indeed.

Most people who work with stock or work on the land have a deep faith, although they may not be 'kirk greedy'. For my part I can't think how anyone who has lived in the country all his working life, and has seen the wonders of nature around him and how it works, could fail to believe in someone greater than man: someone who has given us the changing seasons and all that goes with them, including the promise of 'a seedtime and harvest'. It is a promise that has never been broken in my farming lifetime.

Shepherds have a special place in the 'season of goodwill', from the time when they were watching their flocks by night all those 2,000 years ago. And talking of goodwill at Christmas time, Pat recalls how, as a lad aged seventeen, he was employed to go rabbit trapping. To do this he was staying in a bothy on his own miles from the nearest habitation. He was supplied by a ponyman who came up once a week with his provisions and took away the rabbits, but Pat never once saw him for a much-needed gossip. Pat was there for four months, and came out just before Christmas. He was due quite a bit of money, as the going rate was eightpence (old money) per couple of rabbits, or thirty couple per old pound. He was desperate for the money to pay back his mother who had bought his provisions, and to get a bob or two for a 'spree' after all his lonely nights. But the farm manager, a mean old codger, refused to see him. Eventually Pat was sent for on Christmas Day of all days. The sum due was £25, and as he passed it over the old codger remarked: 'Far too much for a young lad like you.' Hardly the spirit of goodwill!

As I finish off these thoughts and recollections of we three 'oldies', sheep farmers are going through a rough time and some, like Donald's old boss, will go to the wall. But I predict that many more will survive. My heartfelt wish is that they will employ lads who are willing to 'put their boot to the hill' and go on to enjoy a way of life that is second to none—at least it was as far as the 'Three Musketeers' were concerned.

Glossary

ark pig system, outdoor system for pigs: the sow is tethered by a small tin hut and her piglets run free

away-winter, send sheep to lower, better pastures than they would have on the hill for the winter

bonspiel, a curling match

breek, put a garment on a ewe hogg to protect her from the amorous attentions of the tup

bulk (of sheep), a group of twenty-plus

cast (e.g. tup), finished its useful life; too old for the hill

coup, roll over onto back and be unable to rise

cut (e.g. of ewes), group divided from the rest of the sheep

draff, remains of malt after brewing

draft (as in 'draft ewes'), withdrawn from the flock as being unsuitable for further breeding

draw (e.g. cast ewes), select from the flock

fank, enclosure for sheep

gralloch, disembowel

handling, rounding up and penning of sheep and working with them in the fank

haugh, level ground on the banks of a river

heft, group of sheep which have become attached to a particular area of a hill

hirsel, area of hill (larger than a heft) grazed by a flock and looked after by a single shepherd

hogg, young sheep; sheep after the first of January following its birth

horn branded, marked for identification purposes on the horn

keek, glance, look

keel, put owner's mark on sheep; the marking substance itself

knowe, hillock

louping ill, serious sheep disease caused by ticks

lowse (e.g. a horse), unyoke, unharness

luckspenny, money returned to the seller by the buyer as a discount 'for luck'

march, boundary

milk clipping, clipping of the ewes in milk, i.e. those with lambs

mochy, humid, muggy

parrock, small enclosure, usually used for 'setting on' a twin lamb

roughies, sheep which have escaped one or more gatherings and so have not been shorn

rump, eat down to the roots

second draw, sheep of the second grade

A STICK, HILL BOOTS AND A GOOD COLLIE DOG

of quality (the 'tops' are the first
  draw, shotts the third)
shedder, gate for separating sheep
shieling, small area of better grass, used
  in the past as summer grazing for
  cattle, with a hut or cottage for
  temporary use
shott (of lambs), small
speaning, weaning
stell, circular dry-stone enclosure for
  sheep

tup, ram, male sheep

wear (as in 'wear a tup to the shepherd'),
  turn towards, steer in the direction
  of
wedder, wether, castrated ram

yeld (of a ewe), not in lamb